UNDERSTANDING
THE CROSS

By

MALCOLM HEDDING

MAIN STREET BOOKS

UNDERSTANDING THE CROSS

MALCOLM HEDDING

ISBN 978-0-9890173-6-7

Published by:
Main Street Books
Memphis, TN

Printed in USA by The Print Steward.
Grand Rapids, MI

This book is dedicated to Cheryl Hedding, my teenage sweetheart, wife and companion through life. She has been God's very special gift to me and I love her dearly.

Contents

Introduction

The cross of Jesus is vast in its significance. I have often wondered if I am really able to tell others how wonderful it is. As Derek Tidball writes: 'The cross is a wonderfully wrought and complex work of God which cannot be captured in its fullness from one standpoint alone, and even less in theory.' The more one considers what the Bible says about the meaning of the death of Jesus, wonderful highways of thought open up leading this way and that, challenging both heart and life, summonsing repentance and worship from the depths of our beings. We melt before the greatness of the cross. We miss everything if we simply intellectualize about the it – the cross opens to us an experience of God's saving power and insights into the mercy and greatness of God.

Malcolm Hedding's book introduces us to foundational evangelical truth about the cross which invites us to do some meditation of our own and give ourselves to further exploration into the words that cluster around the death of Christ – words such as redemption, propitiation, justification, atonement, reconciliation and others. Then there are also the Old Testament pictures, types and prophecies that give us rich insights into the ministry, death and resurrection of Jesus. As the author himself writes, 'The cross is the central theme of the Bible; it is pictured everywhere in types, symbols, rituals and reality.' The cross is the proof of the extent to which God will go in pursuit of a rebellious world – 'God so loved...'

The prophet Hosea prophesies of the terribly broken relationship between God and Israel. He says to Israel in the opening chapter, 'you are not my people and I am not your God' – a repudiation of the covenant. The covenant has been broken and the threatened curses of the law for unfaithfulness are about to follow – devastating judgements! But then in the eleventh chapter the Lord relents saying, 'I can't do this ....!'

> *"How can I give you up, Ephraim? How can I hand you over, Israel? How can I treat you like Admah? How can I make you like Zeboiim? My heart is changed within me; all my compassion is aroused. I will not carry out my fierce anger, nor will I turn and devastate Ephraim. For I am God, and not man-the Holy One among you. I will not come in wrath.*
> *Hosea 11:8-9*

The point is this: When Jesus was taken from Pilate's judgement hall to Calvary to be nailed there to the cross as the Son of Man, the representative of the whole human race, God went through with it. There was no backing off here. To this extent God loved the world! Jesus suffered our judgement. "He who did not spare his own Son, but gave him up for us all-how will he not also, along with him, graciously give us all things (Romans 8:32)?"

The same is true of the sacrifice of Isaac, for whom Abraham waited twenty-five years. The story in Genesis is full of reminders of Calvary – but then, we have the benefit of hindsight.

'Take your son, your only son, Isaac, whom you love, and go to the region of Moriah. Sacrifice him there as a burnt offering on one of the mountains I will tell you about." The three day journey ... Isaac's questions ... 'God will provide the lamb for the burnt offering, my son'. But God intervened at the final moment and Isaac was replaced by a ram! At Calvary there is no angelic intervention ... just the terrible, anguished cry, 'My God, my God, why have you forsaken me?'

It is something of note to me that the emotions of Abraham are not mentioned in the Genesis account, but we can imagine that he somehow hid the emotional storm from Isaac for three days – and what about the nights? There is no reference to the Father in the crucifixion of Jesus except to His will, His silence and the prayers of Jesus. What was the suffering of the Father?

Did He suffer too? Only the Greeks believed that one of the attributes that the gods required to be a god was 'apatheia' – for us apathy – no feelings! Which is why the idea of a God who loves was so un-godlike as far as Greek philosophers were concerned. Is this perhaps why God calls Abraham 'my friend' and could it be because Abraham, who would not have realized it, shared in the suffering of the Father?

The Trinity was there at Calvary. Hebrews chapter nine refers to Jesus, who through the eternal Spirit, offered himself without spot to God – the suffering Trinity! The wonder is that it is for us.

Dietrich Bonhoeffer wrote, 'God lets himself be pushed out of the world on to the cross ... only the suffering God can help'.

We will never begin to appreciate the vast significance of the cross of Jesus if we have shallow views of the Fall of Humankind – a fall that plunged the universe into the power of decay and handed it all over to evil spirits who oppose God. A kind of human being emerged from that Fall to whom God declared an emphatic 'NO' – a human race that formed a solidarity with the evil one to wrest control of all from the Creator. This kind of being is utterly unacceptable to God. The fallen man is what Paul refers to as 'psuchikos' – the natural man – to whom the things of God are foolishness and not even understandable (1 Corinthians 2:14). These same people are those that Paul describes as dead, dominated by evil powers and by nature are 'objects of wrath' (Ephesians 2:1-3). Adam's race is doomed – it has no future.

But to these same people God declares a welcoming 'YES' to the human race in the reconciling work of Jesus who reconciles the universe to Himself on the cross:

> "... and through him to reconcile to himself all things, whether things on earth or things in heaven, by making peace through his blood, shed on the cross."
> Colossians 1: 20

> "... to be put into effect when the times will have reached their fulfillment - to bring all things in heaven and on earth together under one head, even Christ."
> Ephesians 1:10."

The last Adam is the Head of the New Humanity – changed from 'psuchikos' to 'pneumatikos', the spiritual man who understands the things of God because by the Spirit he is kin to God.

> *"For as in Adam all die, so in Christ all will be made alive."*
> *1 Corinthians 15:22*

> *"So it is written: "The first man Adam became a living being" ; the last Adam, a life-giving spirit."*
> *1 Corinthians 15:45*

Sin is not a small matter – it took omnipotence to deal with it … and defeat it … and issue the invitation to us all to enjoy the fruit of that victory. Like David he stepped onto the battlefield of our humiliation and defeat to destroy a Goliath that had overwhelmed us.

The writer of Hebrews says: 'when he had by himself purged our sins, sat down on the right hand of the Majesty on high; '(Hebrews 1:3). 'By himself' means, 'he alone did it' because only he could do it. And then it also implies 'by means of himself', the Suffering Servant of Isaiah who 'by his knowledge shall justify many; for he shall bear their iniquities' (Isaiah 53:11).

Indeed, this was a fight – a war of universal proportion. The writer of Hebrews states, 'Forasmuch then as the children are partakers of flesh and blood, he also himself likewise took part of the same; that through death he might destroy him that had the power of death, that is, the devil;' (Hebrews 2:14). And Paul writes: 'When you were dead in your sins and in the uncircumcision of your sinful nature, God made you alive with Christ. He forgave us all our sins, having canceled the written code, with its regulations, that was against us and that stood opposed to us; he took it away, nailing it to the cross. And having disarmed the powers and authorities, he made a public spectacle of them, triumphing over them by the cross.' (Colossians 2:13-15).

God has not overlooked sin in bringing us forgiveness. He judged sin in Jesus – the lamb who takes away the sin of the world! The final judgement was brought forward to Calvary. Jesus, speaking to His disciples of His death, said: 'Now is the judgement of this world: now shall the prince of this world be cast out' (John 12:31). This is why he could also say: "I tell you the truth, whoever hears my word and believes him who sent me has eternal life and will not be condemned; he has crossed over from death to life' (John 5:24). This means they will not come into the judgement because the sin of believers in Jesus has been judged at Calvary. This is the Holy Love that Malcolm Hedding speaks of.

At the cross a separation in God, Father and Son, God torn apart in Himself ...'My God, My God, why have you forsaken me?' The moment of his separation from his Father unleashes our reconciliation. Someone once said: 'He bears the burden of his own wrath against us – our sin, under which we would have sunk for all eternity.' Grace is not cheap; it comes at a terrifying cost.

William Temple, Archbishop of Canterbury during the Second World War wrote, 'There cannot be a God of love,' men say, 'because if there was, and he looked upon the world, his heart would break'. The Church points to the cross and says, 'It did break'. 'It's God who made the world' men say. 'It's he who should bear the load'. The Church points to the cross and says, 'He did bear it'.

Of course dying on the cross was part of the journey of Jesus for us. We cannot fail to speak of His resurrection by which He and His work on our behalf is vindicated. As Paul states: 'He was delivered over to death for our sins and was raised to life for our justification.' (Romans 4:25)

Malcolm Hedding's book takes us through a series of wonderful panoramas of the cross of Jesus explaining important terms concerning the work of Christ. Having read it you will be better informed of all that has been accomplished for us; you will be refreshed at heart; you will drawn to the Christ of the cross in gratitude and worship. If you have never given this much thought, a reading of this book will present you with an opportunity and the reason why you should surrender yourself to this Jesus of whom we speak. A hymn written by B. Rhodes:

My heart and voice I raise,
To spread Messiah's praise;
Messiah's praise let all repeat;
The universal Lord,
By whose almighty word
Creation rose in form complete.
A servant's form he wore,

And in His body bore
Our dreadful curse on Calvary:
He like a victim stood,
And poured His sacred blood,
To set the guilty captives free.

But soon the Victor rose
Triumphant o'er His foes,
And led the vanquished host in chains:
He threw their empire down,
His foes compelled to own,
O'er all the great Messiah reigns.

Dr Peter Watt

The Reverend Doctor Peter Watt is the General Chairman of the Assemblies of God of Southern Africa. Peter is an exceptional leader, author, speaker and local Church Pastor. His academic qualifications and wealth of experience in terms of Christian ministry have made him a sought after speaker all over the world. Peter is married to Lesley and they presently reside in Cape Town, South Africa.

Preface

We should remember that when Christ died He was crucified between two sinners. Both were in fact thieves and were rightly condemned but Jesus was sinless and innocent and was actually dying in their place before God. The one thief recognized this and called upon Jesus for help but the other rejected Him and instead mocked Him. Consequently, the one thief died and joined Christ in paradise but the other also died and went to hell. The difference was not what they did but Whom they called upon for salvation.

Over the years I have discovered that Christians have very little knowledge about what actually happened on the cross when Jesus died. Most often they will tell you the obvious in that they will answer your probing question in this regard by saying, "Jesus died for our sins." Which of course is true, but as to why He did this and how the character of God is involved with this they have no idea. Concepts having to do with the biblical terms of propitiation, justification, identification, adoption and sanctification are considered too difficult to grasp and are consequently ignored. In preference they want to hear preaching that makes them feel good and that tells them how much they are loved and cared for by God. As one person once said to me, in echoing this idea, "Why else do we come to Church?"

If this ignorance of what really happened on the cross persists we will breed a generation of Christians that will be biblically illiterate, carnal and of no use to God. More tragic still is the fact that they will never appreciate and value the amazing work of grace and mercy that was accomplished for them when Jesus died on that Roman instrument of execution and rose again from the dead. In addition they will have a view of sin that is inadequate and accepting because they will have no concept of the holiness of God and of His wrath that is unleashed in response to it. Indeed they do not want to hear about the wrath of God and things like this because, as they put it, 'they are far too negative.'

This attitude reveals that many Christians, indeed too many, have an inadequate understanding of the grave consequences of sin. God is opposed, yes vigorously opposed, to sin and to all those who commit it. Sin is evil, very evil, and if not corrected by repentance and faith in what Jesus did on the cross those who practice sin will be visited by the wrath of God. For Paul, we were all sinners and "children of wrath" (Ephesians 2:3) before we came to the cross for deliverance from our sins and their consequences. John tells us that if we do not flee to the cross for deliverance the wrath of God will abide upon us (John 3:36).

The cross is the central theme of the Bible and without it we would not have a Bible and we would be truly lost and doomed. It constitutes a most remarkable demonstration of God's love for a world that has rebelled against Him and which has thereby become His enemies. By it the world, yes everyone in it, has the potential to be justified, put right with God and reconciled to Him (2 Corinthians 5:14-15). Paul determined that it would be the major theme of his preaching and he kept this goal and vision to the day he died (1 Corinthians 2:2). There is thus an urgent need for Christians to understand what really happened when Jesus died for them on the cross and rose again and this short volume seeks to begin this process. I send it forth then in the hope that God, the Holy Spirit, will make its contents a blessing to your life. It is important to note that, in terms of the contents of this book, I have deliberately repeated some of the same truths time and time again in the chapters to follow. I have done this with one goal in mind; to impress upon the reader the importance of really understanding the cross.

Malcolm Hedding

Murfreesboro, Tennessee

CHAPTER I

Before Time Began

"For even the Son of Man did not come to be served, but to serve
and to give His life a ransom for many."
Mark 10:45
"All who dwell on the earth will worship him, whose
names have not been written in the Book of Life of the
Lamb slain from the foundation of the world."
Revelation 13:8

The cross is the central theme of the Bible; it is pictured everywhere in types, symbols, rituals and reality. The Passover story from the book of Exodus is a clear example of this. Leon Morris, in his book, *"The Cross in the New Testament"*, writes, "We begin with Paul's way of finding his teachings in Holy Writ. He was not conscious of being an innovator. He was simply drawing men's attention to what God had revealed and done. He thought of God as active in the atoning work of Christ, and if God was active then God's purpose was being wrought out. Now God had revealed His purpose for men in the pages of the Scripture, so nothing could be more natural for Paul than to find the work of Christ and the way of salvation generally foreshadowed in his Bible. Over and over again he points to the Old Testament to show how the saving events of Christ's life and death were there set forth."

Jesus died on a Roman cross two thousand years ago and this death carries with it a significance and power that can change one's life and eternal destiny forever. It can be said that creation came about because, way back in eternity, before time, space and matter existed, the second person of the Godhead gave His promise that He would come into the world and embrace the cross for the redemption of it. This fact tells us that creation itself, in all its mystery and splendor, could not be put in place without the cross and this is especially true of a created family of men and women that would willingly turn away from sin, submit itself to God and love Him. Without the cross creation would have been still-born! That is, it would have failed in the womb of God's purpose. The cross of Jesus is the cornerstone upon which all of creation was built and Paul acknowledged this when he wrote:

> "In Him we have redemption through His blood, the forgiveness of sins, according to the riches of His grace which He made to abound toward us in all wisdom and prudence, having made known to us the mystery of His will, according to His good pleasure that He purposed in Himself, that in the dispensation of the fullness of the times He might gather together in one all things in Christ, both which are in heaven and which are on earth-in Him."
> Ephesians 1:7-10.

The creation account, recorded in the first chapters of Genesis, tells us that the pinnacle or grand masterpiece of God's creative work is mankind. He is not only the great masterpiece of it but also the very center of it. It exists for him and it will respond to his place in it. This means that should the first man and woman reject God's will and desire for them, as they did, then the glory, wonder and beauty of the world around them would also fall and fail. Mankind's rebellion against God did exactly this and subsequently the created order has fallen; is decaying and is polluted and yet yearning for the day when mankind will again take the position that God originally intended for it. Paul comments on this truth in Romans 8:19-22:

> "For the earnest expectation of the creation eagerly waits for the revelation of the sons of God. For the creation was sub- jected to futility, not willingly, but because of Him who subjected it in hope; because the creation itself also will be delivered from the bondage of corruption into the glorious liberty of the children of God."

The Truth

God could not create a true family for Himself without the fall of mankind. This is so because the creation of a being that could and would think independently from God, even though perfect, meant that such a being would need to know what was the alternative to serving the God that had made it. The Tempter or Serpent simply ignited this question in them by offering them the possibility that something better could be had (Genesis 3:1-7). Our first parents took the gamble and the result was tragic to say the least but indeed, for God, fully expected. A once perfect man and woman would now have to be saved (brought back to a place of fellowship and communion with God) and the only means by which this could be done was the cross of Jesus. God knew this and planned for it before the world began. Consider Paul's words in Ephesians:

> "Blessed be the God and Father of our Lord Jesus Christ, Who has blessed us with every spiritual blessing in the heavenly places in Christ, just as He chose us in Him before the foundation of the world, that we should be holy and without blame before Him in love."
>
> *Ephesians 1:3-4*

The Need

The God of creation and of the Bible is perfect in love and holiness (1 John 4:7). He is "holy-love" meaning that His character cannot abide selfishness or sin; otherwise known as unrighteousness (Habakkuk 1:13). These cannot dwell in His presence and have to be banished and judged; the latter is an expression of His wrath (Romans 1:18). The need that God had and has is that, in dealing with mankind, He also has to satisfy the demands of His character because, if He didn't, He too would become selfish and sinful! Even human judges that fail to dispense proper judgment are accused of corruption and wrong doing; they become like the villains brought before them for judgment. God is no villain and therefore He had to find a way to be just (true to His character) and the justifier (the savior) of sinful and fallen humanity.

So, to sum it all up; the demands of God's character are such that we, all rooted in Adam, had to be removed from His presence eternally, this is death, and placed under His wrath or judgment because of our rebellion against Him. Worse still, we then became prey to the Devil who placed us under his evil dominion. Paul acknowledges this when he writes:

> "And you He made alive, who were dead in trespasses and sins, in which you once walked according to the prince of the power of the air, the spirit who now works in the sons of disobedience, among whom also we all once

conducted ourselves in the lusts of our flesh, fulfilling the desires of the flesh
and of the mind, and were by nature children of wrath, just as the others."
    Ephesians 2:1-3

We need to recognize that the idea that God hates sin and loves the sinner, as preached by many Ministers and Pastors, is theologically incorrect and very dangerous. At face value it appears to be a good thought but actually it totally contradicts the message of the Bible and leaves the hearer with the idea that sin is somehow removed from the sinner making him or her less accountable for it and indeed possibly a victim of it. The truth is, God is intensely set against sinners and He hates them because they are entirely responsible for their actions and accountable to Him for them. They deserve nothing less than His wrath! This is an expression of what we call, "God's holy love." He also loves sinners more than we could ever appreciate and therefore He sent His Son to die for them on the cross but, if they persist in their sinful ways and shun His great love, God Himself will send His wrath upon them and banish them forever to hell. William Temple writes, " Sin is not an accretion (growth) attached to my real life; it is myself, as that self now exists. He loves me even while I sin; but it cannot be said too strongly that there is a wrath of God against me as sinning; God's will is set one way and mine is set against it. There is a collision of wills; and God's will is not passive in that collision."

So hell is a very real place, initially prepared by God for the Devil and his angels (Matthew 25:41), and according to Jesus, is characterized by "outer darkness" (Matthew 25:30), flames of fire and a strange worm that wraps itself around those that end up there forever. Jesus definitely warns that a God who is essentially love will send unrepentant sinners there.

> *"But I will show you whom you should fear: Fear Him who, after He has*
> *killed, has power to cast into hell; yes, I say fear Him!"*
>   *Luke 5:12*

> *"If your hand causes you to sin, cut it off. It is better for you to enter into life*
> *maimed, rather than having two hands to go to hell, into the fire that shall nev-*
> *er be quenched- where 'Their worm does not die and the fire is not quenched."*
>   *Mark 9:43-44*

Jesus took the sinner's place on the cross and His awful sufferings, like those of hell, are a picture of what we deserve; nothing less. In fact scripture tells us that His body was so badly disfigured by the abuse heaped upon it that its basic form was no longer recognizable. This was the price that God in Christ had to pay to redeem us!

> *"Just as many were astonished at you, so His visage was marred more than any man, and His form more than the sons of men; So shall He sprinkle many nations."*
> *Isaiah 52:14-15*

Truly, as the hymn writer noted, when we gaze upon the cross, we should tremble and respond by true repentance fully recognizing that in fact Jesus' death, with all its agony and suffering, was what we deserved as sinners. He was literally cursed of God!

All this means that we were truly lost and could not find our way back to God because:

We cannot re-embrace His perfection no matter how hard we may try. Even our best efforts cannot bring us close to the glory of God's character (Romans 3:23). Our good works will just not save us and thus, in terms of salvation, they become dead works (useless and without merit before God) that in fact have to be repented of (Hebrews 6:1-2)! In his Ephesian letter Paul reinforces this truth when he writes:

> *"For by grace you have ben saved through faith, and that not of yourselves; it is the gift of God, not of works lest anyone should boast."*
> *Ephesians 2:8-9*

We could not "get out of jail", as it were, after serving our prison term because the term is eternal; in that "the wages of sin is death" (Romans 6:23) and death is a state of eternal separation from God (2 Thessalonians 1:6-9). In short we were dead, children of wrath, without hope and doomed (Ephesians 2:1-3). We were then forever cursed of God (Galatians 3:10).

The reality of all of this is that we can do nothing to save ourselves and if we live a good life, as we see it, we will still be separated from God's presence forever (Ephesians 2:8). Also, we cannot find a champion amongst ourselves who will breach this chasm between God and mankind because all of mankind is in the "same boat." When this truth dawned upon the Apostle John we are told that he wept (Revelation 5:1-4). The need that God has is to be true to His character and at the same time merciful to us. Even the prophets of old and the angels, knowing well this dilemma, could not envisage a solution to it:

> *"Of this salvation the prophets have inquired and searched carefully, who prophesied of the grace that would come to you, searching what, or what manner of time, the Spirit of Christ who was in them was indicating when He testified beforehand the sufferings of Christ and the glories that would follow.To them it was revealed that, not to themselves, but to us they were ministering the things which now have been reported to you through those who have preached to you by the Holy Spirit sent from heaven-things which angels desire to look into."*
> *1 Peter 1:10-12*

The Solution

A savior could not be found and cannot be found on earth from amongst mankind and yet God knew all of this would transpire before He made the world. He thus also knew, before the foundation of the world that He would have to become the solution to sin's problem if He wanted to gain a family with which He could live eternally. He thus decided in Jesus, the second person of the Godhead, to come into the world and thereby be incarnated in a human body:

> *"And the Word became flesh and dwelt among us, and we beheld His glory as of the only begotten of the Father, full of grace and truth."*
> *John 1:14*

Paul put it this way:

> *"...God was in Christ reconciling the world to Himself not imputing their trespasses to them..."*
> *2 Corinthians 5:19*

This "New Adam" (1Corinthians 15:45) would be fully God and fully man and being without sin He could and did die for all of humanity as their representative. He died in our place and for our sins and thus satisfied the demands of God's character against us (1 Peter 3:18). His death was therefore substitutionary (in the place of) and a propitiation, meaning that it fully satisfied and placated the character of God on our behalf. God could be true to His character and have mercy upon us. Paul put it this way:

"...for all have sinned and fall short of the glory of God, being justified freely by His grace through the redemption that is in Christ Jesus, whom God set forth as a propitiation by His blood, through faith, to demonstrate His righteousness, because in His, forbearance God had passed over the sins that were previously committed, to demonstrate at the present time His righteousness, that He might be just and the justifier of the one who has faith in Jesus."
Romans 3:23-26

"Much more then, having now been justified by His blood, we shall be saved from wrath through Him."
Romans 5:9

Peter wrote of Christ's death in these terms:
"For Christ also suffered once for sins, the just for the unjust, that He might bring us to God, being put to death in the flesh but made alive by the Spirit."
1 Peter 3:18

All this being true the cross is changed from an awful instrument of execution to a glorious symbol of hope and salvation. Its meaning becomes greater than the events surrounding it and thus, as Jesus cried out from it, "Tetelestai" meaning, "It is finished" or more correctly "it is paid", we recognize that our debt has been paid in full and that God our Creator has found a way not only to save us (to justify and thereby declare us legally free from the consequences of our sin and rebellion against Him) but to demonstrate that He truly is holy-love and can be trusted for eternity (John 3:16) (1 John 4:10). We embrace this with joy and become what He desired us to be before time began, His children! Truly Jesus became our "kinsman redeemer" (a Savior from amongst us) and because of His perfect and sinless life He could lay it down for us and pick it up again by the resurrection; a testimony to His divinity (Romans 1:3-4). The resurrection of Jesus is proof that our sins have been fully atoned for. It is only by grace, God's unmerited favor that we have been saved from the penalty we deserved for our sins. Our good works are just like filthy rags before Him and our only hope is what Christ did for us on the cross.

> *"But we are all like an unclean thing, all our righteousnesses are like filthy rags; we all fade as a leaf, and our iniquities, like the wind have taken us away."*
> Isaiah 64:6

In essence God provided a new beginning for us in Christ, the new Adam (1 Corinthians 15:22). If we attach our lives to Him we become everything that God wanted us to be from eternity but if we remain attached to the old Adam, by rejecting His redeeming love in Christ, we shall die with him in our sins. Paul expressed this truth in this way:

> *"For as by one man's disobedience many were made sinners, so also by one Man's obedience many will be made righteous."*
> Romans 5:19

> And; *"For since by man came death, by Man also came the resurrection of the dead. For as in Adam all die, even so in Christ all shall be made alive."*
> 1 Corinthians 15:21-22

Another way of understanding this is the following: The human race that came out of Adam, and was thus in him, has been put to death. It is dead and buried by the death and burial of Jesus having been entirely summed up in Him and judged. However, by Jesus' resurrection, a new race of men and women has come out of Him. This new race is deemed perfect and righteous and will be made perfect by Christ's life in it and it will dwell with God eternally. The question is, which Adam do we come out of? If the answer is only Adam then we will die and thus be separated from God for all eternity but if indeed it is Christ Jesus, the "New Adam", then we will live and share His eternal glory in the New Jerusalem coming out of heaven. In short, the worm must die in the grave of the cocoon and come forth from this place of death as a beautiful butterfly; an entirely different creature. Paul said, "If any man be in Christ He is a new creation, the old things have passed away; behold all things have become new." (2 Corinthians 5:17)

The way home to God is only via the cross of Jesus and we rightly embrace it by repenting of our wickedness and trusting fully in the finished work done upon it by Jesus on our behalf. There is no other way of salvation (Acts 4:12). Paul described this glorious gift of salvation thus:

> *"And you being dead in your trespasses and the uncircumcision of your flesh, He has made alive together with Him, having forgiven you all trespasses, having wiped out the handwriting of requirements that was against us, which was contrary to us. And He has taken it out of the way, having nailed it to the cross."*
> *Colossians 2:13-14*

The picture here of the cross is a graphic one indeed in that, in Roman times, when a criminal was executed on a cross his crimes were written out and nailed over the cross so that all could see why he was being put to death. All our sins, past, present and future, were nailed to Jesus' cross in like manner and we then, by His death in our place, are freed from all of them. This is amazing grace! Isaiah, reflecting on these great and holy things wrote:

> *"Surely he has borne our griefs and carried our sorrows; yet we esteemed Him stricken, smitten by God, and afflicted. But He was wounded for our transgressions He was bruised for our iniquities; the chastisement for our peace was upon Him, and by His stripes we are healed. All we like sheep have gone astray; we have turned, every one, to his own way; and the Lord has laid on Him the iniquity on us all."*
> *Isaiah 53:4-6*

David Pawson, commenting on Christ's sufferings writes, "We can put it this way: When Jesus in the last three hours on the cross was in darkness, was thirsty, was desperately lonely, that is what hell is like. In hell, you are in darkness; in hell you are lonely; in hell you are thirsty-it is a hot place." All of this reminds us that Christ's sufferings were physical and spiritual. On the cross, God His Father turned His back on Him and utterly forsook Him. This is why Jesus cried out, "My God, My God why have You forsaken Me" (Mark 15:34).

The Choice

Our response to the grace and love of God in Christ should be that of real repentance for our sins and of faith in Jesus' finished work on the cross. We should make Jesus Lord of our lives and consequently God our Father will declare us to be righteous just like Jesus is righteous. That is, He will justify us (declare our legal obligations before Him to have been fully met) and we will be declared guilty but now fully forgiven and henceforth treated by Him as if we had never sinned. The penalty (wrath of God) for all our sins, past, present and future, will be removed from us thereby freeing us from all condemnation. Our Father in heaven will reconcile us to Himself and bring us into a living and real relationship with Himself by Jesus Christ. By the Holy Spirit He will stamp assurance of these things upon our hearts so that we will know that we know that we are saved and have eternal life (Romans 8:16). Romans five sets forth the blessings of being justified by God's grace in Christ:

> *"Therefore, having been justified by faith, we have peace with god through our Lord Jesus Christ, through whom also we have access by faith into this grace in which we stand, and we rejoice in the hope of the glory of God. And not only that, but we also glory in tribulations, knowing that tribulation produces perseverance; and perseverance, character; and character, hope. Now hope does not disappoint, because the love of God has been poured out in our hearts by the Holy Spirit who was given to us."*
> *Romans 5:1-5*

We note from this passage that by Christ's atonement on the cross we are:

Reconciled to God
Have peace with Him
Are filled with Joy…and we are,
Given real hope, even in great trials, by the Holy Spirit Who lives in us.

Our Savior fully satisfied the demands of God's character on our behalf and thereby secured for each one of us the gift of God's righteousness (2 Corinthians 5:21). The Bible states that He tasted death for every man and this constitutes the glory and reach of the cross (Hebrews 2:9). No one need perish eternally for "God is not willing that any should perish"(2 Peter 3:9) and to celebrate this truth the veil in the Temple was split from the top to the bottom when Jesus died (Matthew 27:51). God, in Christ, literally came down from heaven and filled our hearts with His love and blessing. The Bible calls the reception of this love and blessing being born again or regenerated by the Holy Spirit (John 3:3; Titus 3:4-6). Those who embrace God's saving grace in the cross will begin an eternal adventure with Him but those who reject this great saving work of the cross will be forever banished from the presence of God (2 Thessalonians 1:9) and have their abode in hell; a place once only prepared for the Devil and his angels (Matthew 25:41). Given this remarkable story of God's love for sinful men and women the following verses, taken from Isaiah 53, take on new meaning:

"Yet it pleased the Lord to bruise Him; He has put Him to grief. When You make His soul an offering for sin, He shall see His seed, He shall prolong His days, and the pleasure of the Lord shall prosper in His hand. He shall see the labor of His soul, and be satisfied. By His knowledge My righteous Servant shall justify many, for He shall bear their iniquities."

However, it is important to note that the evidence of sin is alienation. That is, alienation from God and from our fellow man or woman. Sin separates us from one another, makes us selfish and causes destruction everywhere in our relationships. When we are justified by faith and reconciled to God through the cross this selfish principle in our lives is broken and we should be reconciled to all those in our world regardless of their race, color, social standing, creed and position. This is the abiding evidence that the love of God has conquered our sinful hearts by the cross. So, Paul writes:

"For you are all sons of God through faith in Christ Jesus. For as many of you as were baptized into Christ have put on Christ. There is neither Jew nor Greek, there is neither slave or free, there is neither male nor female; for you are all one in Christ Jesus."
Galatians 3:26-28

Given this reality, this is why Christians should not have broken relationships, as these are evidence of a carnal unsaved heart. We must make it our business to be at peace with all men and Paul put it this way:

"If it is possible, as much as depends on you, live peaceably with all men."
Romans 12:18

In fact, in all of his epistles Paul constantly calls upon his readers to live at peace with one another, to embrace unity, to be tenderhearted, forgiving and of one mind. The cross of Jesus definitely breaks the power of alienation and division in our hearts and those who continue to practice these in the community of faith are to be rejected because they are quite honestly not saved!

> *"Reject a divisive man after the first and second warning, knowing that such a person is warped and sinning, being self condemned."*
> *Titus 3:10-11*

> *"Now I urge you, brethren, note those who cause divisions and offences, contrary to the doctrine which you learned, and avoid them."*
> *Romans 16:17*

The "doctrine which you learned" is that of the cross of Jesus that if properly embraced reconciles us to God and man and brings us into a state of peace in both spheres. This reality, according to Paul, is evidence that we have been truly saved. Christians live in peace with God and with man and so, as regards our interaction with one another, Paul has this to say in his Ephesian letter:

> *"I, therefore, the prisoner of the Lord, beseech you to walk worthy of the calling with which you were called, with all lowliness and gentleness, with long suffering, bearing with one another in love, endeavoring to keep the unity of the Spirit in the bond of peace."*
> *Ephesians 4:1-3*

CHAPTER 2

Being Saved by His Life

"I have been crucified with Christ; it is no longer I who live, but Christ lives in me; and the life which I now live in the flesh I live by faith in the Son of God, who loved me and gave Himself for me."
Galatians 2:20

In our previous study we examined the nature of Jesus' atoning work on the cross. In short, because of His sinless and perfect life Jesus could lay His life down as a satisfying atonement for the sins of the world and take it up again. Death could not hold Him because of His perfect and therefore indestructible, or endless, life (Hebrews 7:16). The resurrection of Jesus was the ultimate and abiding evidence of this and of the fact that he was God Himself in the flesh. He was therefore able to pay the price for sinners and, by His resurrection life, able to infuse them with His saving power or, as the writer of the book of Hebrews states, save us to the "uttermost". It is important to note that this atoning sacrifice for sinners was a once for all, all-sufficient work that does not need repeating (Hebrews 9:27-28). The sinner is thus not only declared righteous, that is, God imputes or gives to his credit righteousness as a gift, but actually is made righteous. That is, righteousness is imparted to him. Paul underlines this in his letter to the Church at Rome when he writes:

"Much more then, having now been justified by His blood, we shall be saved from wrath through Him. For if when we were enemies we were reconciled to God through the death of His Son, much more, having been reconciled, we shall be saved by His life."
Romans 5:9-10

Being saved by Jesus' life is what the Bible calls being sanctified; which in turn can be defined as that ongoing work of the Holy Spirit in us by which the effects of sin upon our characters are reversed. By this cleansing process our evil nature is put to death or eradicated and we begin to reflect once again the image of God or as Peter put it "the divine nature" (2 Peter 1:4). Again Paul refers to this process in these ways:

"But we are bound to give thanks to God always for you, brethren beloved by the Lord, because God from the beginning chose you for salvation through sanctification by the Spirit and belief in the truth."
2 Thessalonians 2:13

"But of Him you are in Christ Jesus, who became for us wisdom from God-and righteousness and sanctification and redemption."
1 Corinthians 1:30

Those who faithfully walk with God by Jesus Christ are thereby embracing what the Bible calls holiness and without this we shall not see the Lord (Hebrews 12:14). In other words; when Jesus said that we are to pick up the cross and follow Him (Matthew 16:24), He meant that we are to embrace everything that His cross purchased for us and chiefly this means that we are not only reconciled to God but that we are also, by the indwelling power of the Holy Spirit, made to be actually righteous. Righteousness is imparted to us and so we are changed from within to reflect the character of Christ. We therefore allow His Spirit to cleanse us from sin or eradicate the strongly entrenched "I" or selfish principle in us. The Bible calls this "I principle" being fleshly or carnal (1 Corinthians 3:1-3) and it also designates it the "old man":

"But you have not so learned Christ, if indeed you have heard Him and have been taught by Him, as the truth is in Jesus: that you put off, concerning your former conduct, the old man which grows corrupt according

to deceitful lusts, and be renewed in the spirit of your mind, and that
you put on the new man which was created according to God, in true
righteousness and holiness."
    Ephesians 4:20-24

It is then important to note that the cross of Jesus did not open up a way for man to get out of hell into heaven, but rather, it opened up a way for God to get out of heaven into man and so as a consequence we are delivered from hell. Allowing God by Christ Jesus to invade our lives is the ultimate purpose of God and it is the major issue facing every Christian. This is what it means to be a fully devoted follower of Christ. By the cross of Jesus we have been reconciled to God our Father and so; being a disciple of Jesus means that we allow God to fully transform our lives until they reflect as closely as possible, on this side of the grave, the character of God. This process of progressive transformation the Bible calls sanctification. Paul put it this way:

"For whom He foreknew, He also predestined to be conformed to the
image of His Son, that He might be the firstborn among many brethren."
    Romans 8:29

In the end, when Jesus comes a second time, our bodies, souls and spirits will be sanctified completely and we shall be like Him. Paul affirms that this is indeed the will of God when he writes:

"Now may the God of peace Himself sanctify you completely; and may
your whole spirit, soul, and body be preserved blameless at the coming
of our Lord Jesus Christ."
    1 Thessalonians 5:23

And John writes:

"...but we know that when He is revealed, we shall be like Him, for we
shall see Him as He is."
    1 John 3:2

So, the goal of Jesus' death and resurrection was to create men and women, a family if you will, who would willingly love God, serve God and reflect His image for all eternity. The cross of Jesus is the only means by which

God can create such a family. We are therefore created in Christ Jesus and are thus trophies of His workmanship. Once again Paul acknowledges this truth by writing:

> *"For by grace you have been saved through faith, and that not of your-selves; it is the gift of God, not of works, lest anyone should boast. For we are His workmanship, created in Christ Jesus for good works, which God prepared beforehand that we should walk in them."*
> *Ephesians 2:8-10*

The Loving Power of Christ in Us

The difference between defeat and victory depends on the follower of Jesus having a good grasp of what has really happened to him because of the cross of Jesus. That is, he or she must understand the nature of the incredible power that flows toward them by being in Christ. The love of God embracing us is immeasurable and the power of God in us unassailable. This means that there is no power in heaven, on earth or under the earth that can overcome the loving and transforming power and protection of God; which is ours (Romans 8:38-39). Paul recognized that the followers of Jesus needed a revelation (heart understanding) of this truth:

> *"Therefore I also, after I heard of your faith in the Lord Jesus and your love for all the saints, do not cease to give thanks for you, making men-tion of you in my prayers: that the God of our Lord Jesus Christ, the Father of glory, may give to you the spirit of wisdom and revelation in the knowledge of Him, the eyes of your understanding being enlightened; that you may know what is the hope of His calling, what are the riches of the glory of His inheritance in the saints, and what is the exceeding greatness of His power toward us who believe, according to the working of His mighty power which He worked in Christ when He raised Him from the dead and seated Him at His right hand in the heavenly places, far above all principality and power and might and dominion, and every name that is named, not only in this age but also in that which is to come."*
> *Ephesians 2:15-21*

It will be noted from this passage, and it cannot be repeated often enough, that the follower of Jesus is infused with a power in Christ that is greater than any principality (demonic entity), earthly kingdom, any living entity or person in this age and the one to come. Peter affirms this in his second epistle when he states that by virtue of knowing Christ or being in Him "we have everything we need for life and godliness" (2 Peter 1:3). Given that this is true, why do so many Christians struggle and fail? Also, the believer in Jesus is immersed in a "sea of God's love" that is knowable but not exhaustible. That is, it can be experienced, but is just too great to be fully grasped or known!

> *"For this reason I bow my knees to the Father of our Lord Jesus Christ, from whom the whole family in heaven and earthed is named, that He would grant you, according to the riches of His glory, to be strengthened with might through His Spirit in the inner man, that Christ may dwell in your hearts through faith; that you being rooted and grounded in love, may be able to comprehend with all the saints what is the width and length and depth and height-to know the love of Christ which passes knowledge; that you may be filled with all the fullness of God."*
> *Ephesians 3:14-19*

Again, the Jesus follower is to comprehend and be assured of the great love that God in Christ has for him. There is therefore no limit to knowing God's love just as there is no limit to knowing God's transforming power. The sin factor in our lives is broken, the Devil has no power over us and the world has no lure; all because of the cross of Jesus. Leon Morris in his book, "The Cross in the New Testament" writes, "In the preceding chapter (Romans 7) we noticed that Paul sees man as caught up in a grim and many-sided bondage. Over against that we must now notice that he sees the cross as an act of deliverance on a grand scale. Whatever tyrants lord it over man, their power is broken by Christ's atoning work." Paul is more than clear about all of this but so many Christians know nothing of these blessings; why? Because they need to grasp the five key biblical principles of:

1. Identification
We died in Christ and consequently we rose with Christ and we are now seated in heavenly places with Christ. His death, burial and resurrection is ours and thus by the exceeding great power and love of God we are already in heaven! Such is the grace of God flowing toward us. Again, Leon Morris writes, "The believer and the Christ are in the closest possible connection. If it is true that their death is made His death, it is also true that His death

is made their death." Christ in us is an "incredible thing" as it is the "hope of glory". That is, the means by which we attain to the perfection of His character. Paul knowing this says:

"I have been crucified with Christ; it is no longer I who live, but Christ lives in me; and the life which I now live in the flesh I live by faith in the Son of God, who loved me and gave Himself for me."
Galatians 2:20

"But God, who is rich in mercy, because of His great love with which He loved us, even when we were dead in trespasses, made us alive together with Christ...and raised us up together, and made us sit together in the heavenly places in Christ Jesus..."
Ephesians 2:4-6

For God the power unleashed at the cross is such that it instantly completed the great work of salvation in us. We simply have to walk this out in time and through the days allotted to us; all the while knowing that we cannot possibly fail habitually. By the grace of God then, we make our heavenly position an earthly reality. Paul called this, pursuing the "upward call of God in Christ Jesus" in that we are to see ourselves as already perfect in heaven and thus we set out day by day to make this true of our reality:

"Not that I have already attained, or am already perfected; but I press on, that I may lay hold of that for which Christ Jesus has also laid hold of me. Brethren, I do not count myself to have apprehended; but one thing I do, forgetting those things which are behind and reaching forward to those which are ahead, I press toward the goal for the prize of the upward call of God in Christ Jesus.
Philippians 3:12-14

Secondly, to walk with Jesus, as we should we need to know the principle of:

2. Perception

The barrier preventing us from reaching God's powerful deliverance in and of our lives is ourselves or what we call our minds. Your mind is the real you but the effects of sin have darkened our imaginations or minds (Ephesians

4:17-18) leaving the seat of our very being crippled and unable to agree with God. When this barrier is torn down by submission to Jesus' lordship and by earnest prayer and devotion our minds are made submissive to God and transformation is the result. This must be our daily cry to God; we have the power and love of God to change, all we require is the "will." Our perception of God's ability to transform us has to change. We must believe that He can change us and will if we let Him. Paul well knew the nature of this struggle and therefore recognized that the rebellious nature of our thoughts can keep us from appropriating God's will for our lives and so he stated that by earnest and believing prayer he would cast "down arguments and every high thing that exalts itself against the knowledge of God..." (2 Corinthians 10:5). With the same thought in mind Paul pens these words in his Roman letter:

> *"I beseech you therefore, brethren, by the mercies of God, that you present your bodies a living sacrifice holy, acceptable to God, which is your reasonable service. And do not be conformed to this world, but be transformed by the renewing of your mind, that you may prove what is that good and acceptable and perfect will of God."*
> *Romans 12:1-2*

Peter also recognized that Christian transformation begins with our minds and therefore he commanded his readers to, "Gird up the loins of your minds" (1 Peter 1:13). Here the mind is seen as a belt that if not properly worn will cause your pants to fall down! The lesson is clear, when we submit our minds to Christ's will for our lives we change by His power in us and our spiritual pants don't fall down. (See also: Ephesians 4:20-24)

The Christ follower must recognize, have the perception or understanding continuously, that he has the capacity to change and therefore he must reckon himself to be dead indeed to sin, "but alive to God in Christ Jesus our Lord" (Romans 6:11). Paul put it this way:

> *"Therefore do not let sin reign in your mortal body, that you should obey it in its lusts. And do not present your members as instruments of unrighteousness to sin, but present yourselves as instruments of righteousness to God. For sin shall not have dominion (power) over you..."*
> *Romans 6:12-14*

Then we need to know the principle of:

3. Injection

When we gave our lives to Christ, because of what He did for us on the cross, something wonderful actually happened to us in that we were regenerated by His Spirit and given a real hunger and thirst for God. To put it another way; we were born again (John 3:3) and from within we experienced something amazing. In short, we were actually injected with God's real power, love and presence. John writes of this fact by stating that when we came to faith God placed the seed of His life within us (1 John 3:9). If you have never had this experience then, to be honest, you have never been saved and your life remains under His wrath (John 3:36)! Paul, writing to Titus described this experience thus:

> *"But when the kindness and the love of God our Savior toward man appeared, not by works of righteousness which we have done, but according to His mercy He saved us, through the washing of regeneration and renewing of the Holy Spirit, whom He poured out on us abundantly through Jesus Christ our Savior."*
> *Titus 3:4-6*

All this means that you now know that the greatest power in the universe has impacted your life and empowered it because of the cross; meaning that now you can build on this injection and allow it to fully transform your life. There can be no other outcome! Once again the Apostle John recognizing this great truth writes:

> *"You are of God, little children and have overcome them, because He who is in you is greater than he who is in the world."*
> *1 John 4:4*

It is certainly therefore true that we have received "everything we need for life and godliness in Christ Jesus "(2 Peter 1:3). It is now for us to expand God's presence and power in our lives by exposing ourselves to the means by which this can happen. That is, we need to attend a good Bible believing church, cultivate good prayer lives, spend much time in His word, enjoy stimulating Christian fellowship and frequently recall His goodness to us by the breaking of bread or communion. This was the "pattern" laid down for us by the early church.

> *"Then those who gladly received his word were baptized; and that day about three thousand souls were added to them. And they continued steadfastly in the apostles doctrine and fellowship, in the breaking of bread, and in the prayers."*
> *Acts 2:41-42*

Those who expose themselves to the real life of God by these regular godly pursuits will experience the full power of the cross cascading through their lives and they will be a blessing to the world. Most of all they will be transformed to reflect the very image of Christ:

> *"And He Himself gave some to be apostles, some prophets, some evangelists, and some pastors and teachers, for the equipping of the saints for the work of the ministry, for the edifying of the body of Christ, till we all come to the unity of the faith and of the knowledge of the Son of God, to a perfect man, to the measure of the stature of the fullness of Christ.."*
> *Ephesians 4:11-13*

In addition we need to say something about:

4. Failure

Grappling with our sinful natures is not easy and so, while the cross has made full provision for our victory, we continue to struggle with our inability to give God the full submission and obedience that He demands. The result is we all continue to fail and sin. In fact John, in his first epistle writes, "if we say we do not sin we lie and the truth is not in us" (1 John 1:8). So, for sure, we do not wish to sin but we do and this should concern us because we retard our spiritual growth thereby and offend the heart of God. More important still, it should drive us quickly to confession and repentance. In this regard John writes:

> *"If we confess our sins, He is faithful and just to forgive us our sins and to cleanse us from all unrighteousness."*
> *1 John 1:9*

It is important to note that we should not allow sinful habits to form in our lives again as this will seriously challenge our spiritual progress and could even seriously damage it. The sins that we commit need to be immediately repented of and should never be allowed to become habitual. If this happens it constitutes a serious denial of the power of the cross and it raises questions about the real nature of one's commitment to Jesus and relationship with Him. The true believer in Jesus is consumed with love for God and gratefulness for what He has done for him in Christ and so; having such a wonderful hope, he "purifies himself, just as He is pure" (1 John 3:3). Thus it is that John once again writes:

> "Whoever has been born of God does not sin, for His seed remains in him; and he cannot sin, because he has been born of God."
> 1 John 3:9

Here John is not contradicting his previous statement in the same epistle. Indeed not; as he is merely stating that true Christians do not sin habitually. Christ, by His presence in them, has cancelled the power of sin in them and so, if anything; they walk in righteousness (1 John2: 29). The true Christ follower keeps short accounts with God when he fails and he thereby overcomes the power of sin in his life. He does not let the "sun go down on his anger" (Ephesians 4:26). Jesus knows our frailty, He is full of compassion and love and will help us and forgive us when we fail but we have to become "Overcomers" and this is the challenge of walking with Him.

> "He who overcomes shall be clothed in white garments and I will not blot out his name from the Book of Life; but I will confess his name before My Father and before His angels."
> Revelation 3:5

5. Adoption

The biblical teaching on justification, sanctification and identification all have to do with the standing and power that God gives us as children of God. However, the subject of "Adoption" introduces us to the amazing love and destiny that God by Jesus Christ has for each one of us. It draws us into an understanding of His Fatherhood and introduces us to what it really means to be a part of His family. Consider then the following verses of scripture:

"For you did not receive the spirit of bondage again to fear, but you received the Spirit of adoption by whom we cry out, 'Abba, Father."
    Romans 8:15

"But when the fullness of the time had come, God sent forth His Son, born of a woman, born under the law, to redeem those who were under the law, that we might receive the adoption as sons."
    Galatians 4:4-5

Paul's understanding of the subject of adoption is rooted in his knowledge and experience of the Roman slave market of his day. Slaves were held in cages, they were totally enslaved to their slave traders and masters and they had no rights at all as they were seen only as commodities and not even as human beings. They could consequently be abused, cruelly treated and even murdered with impunity. They had a life that was wretched and tormenting to say the least and fear was their only friend!

For Paul then, Jesus, the true born literal begotten Son of the Father, walked into the slave market, saw us entrapped in our cages and in our miserable bondage and fear, and bought us at great price. He then, having purchased us, freed us from our shackles and then brought us into His Father's presence; Who bestowed upon us the same rights and privileges as the Son by birth. This means that God adopted us, made us His own and shared Jesus' inheritance equally with us; just as if we were his own natural born children. We have become "joint-heirs" with Christ!

"The Spirit Himself bears witness with our spirit that we are children of God, and if children, then heirs-heirs of God and joint heirs with Christ, if indeed we suffer with Him, that we may also be glorified together."
    Romans 8:16-17

It is because of this remarkable adoptive action of God that scripture declares that we shall reign with Christ over the world in the Messianic Age or one thousand year reign of Jesus over the nations. Indeed we shall sit with Him on His throne and all because we are joint-heirs with Him!

"To him who overcomes I will grant to sit with Me on My throne, as I

also overcame and sat with My Father on His throne."
Revelation 3:21

And then scripture pulls back the veil a little more and lets us into another mystery that is equally amazing. John the apostle tells us in his first epistle that, "Now we are children of God; and it has not yet been revealed what we shall be, but we know that when He is revealed, we shall be like Him, for we shall see Him as He is (John 3:2)." In other words, our Father has a destiny for us, together with Christ, that is still a secret but part of the amazing love that He has bestowed upon us as His children. If ever there was a story of "from rags to riches' then this is it but in this case in consists of, "from the slave cage in the market of sin to the very throne of God." This is all because of the cross of Jesus.

CHAPTER 3

Walking in the Spirit

"I say then: Walk in the Spirit, and you shall
not fulfill the lust of the flesh."
Galatians 5: 16

"Now all things are of God, who has reconciled us to Him-
self through Jesus Christ, and has given us the ministry of
reconciliation, that is, that God was in Christ reconcil-
ing the world to Himself, not imputing their trespasses to
them and has committed to us the word of reconciliation."
2 Corinthians 5:18-19

The cross of Jesus reconciles our lives to the God of heaven. It makes us compatible with His perfect character and enables Him to be on our side and to invade our lives with His transforming power. This remarkable demonstration of God's love, power and grace frees us from the fear of disapproval, condemnation and judgment. We are fully "accepted in the Beloved" (Ephesians 1:6) and covered with His righteousness. We are the righteousness of God in Christ (2 Corinthians 5:21). This is amazing and good news indeed. John wrote of this new standing that we have before God in this way:

"Love has been perfected among us in this: that we may have boldness
in the day of judgment; because as He is, so are we in this world. There
is no fear in love; but perfect feat casts out fear, because fear involves

torment. But he who fears has not been made perfect in love. We Love him because He first loved us."
   1 John 4:17-19

And Paul wrote of our new standing before God in this way:

"Blessed be the God and Father of our Lord Jesus Christ, who has blessed us with every spiritual blessing in the heavenly places in Christ, just as He chose us in Him before the foundation of the world, that we should be holy and without blame before Him in love."
   Ephesians 1:3-4

As Christians we need to know these facts and live by them. It is precisely here that we fail and all of Paul's letters are written with this goal in mind. That is, with the goal in mind of every person who has repented of his or her sins and made Jesus Lord of their lives becoming everything that Jesus' death, burial and resurrection purchased for them. So, this means that we need:

To Learn to Come Into God's Presence
The writer of the book of Hebrews tells us that we need to do this boldly.

"Let us therefore come boldly to the throne of grace, that we may obtain mercy and find grace to help in time of need."
   Hebrews 4:16

We come into God's presence boldly on the grounds of what Jesus did for us on the cross. We are not deterred from doing this because of some earthly experience relating to our natural fathers etc. God is our Father and He is like none other and when Jesus saves us He brings us into a right relationship with His Father. Jesus' blood, the evidence of His death for sinners, gives us unhindered and full access to God our Father (Hebrews 10:19). We are justified by Jesus' spilt blood and are subsequently in right standing with God our Father Who now has absolutely nothing against us. This is vital truth and it needs to be stamped on our hearts by the Holy Spirit. It is therefore our understanding of what happened on the cross that propels us with joy into the very throne room of God! It is when we are assured of these things that we will exercise our right to approach God our Father free from doubts and fears. The truth of God will set you free from these and this is precisely why we need to live in God's word (John 8:31-32). Also, it is ignorance, doubt, condemnation and fear that keep us from boldly coming into God's presence by prayer. The truth is, it is by praying, just talking to God in Jesus' name that we draw near to God and find His comfort. Jesus called this abiding in Him (John 15:4) and for those who do so He gave this promise:

> *"And whatever you ask in My name, that will I do, that the father may*
> *be glorified in the Son. If you ask any thing in My name, I will do it."*
> *John 14:13-14*

To Learn to Trust the Power of Christ in Us

The Bible affirms that it is Christ in us the hope of glory (Colossians 1:27). That is, Jesus transforming power inside each one of us can change us into a reflection of the character of God. There is no power on earth that can stand in the way of Jesus' work in us because "greater is He that is in us than he that is in the world" (1 John 4:4). This in turn means that the ungodly habits, actions and addictions of our lives have all been conquered by the cross. There is no need for us to be entrapped by any of them. This, in itself is a revelation that has to be fully grasped by us. Until we thoroughly learn this truth we shall continue to be held captive by defeated tormentors! It is thus precisely because of Jesus' great power residing in us that we can truly consider ourselves to be dead to sin; unresponsive to it. Paul affirmed this when he wrote:

> *"Likewise you also, reckon yourselves to be dead indeed to sin, but alive*
> *to God in Christ Jesus our Lord. Therefore do not let sin reign in your*
> *mortal body, that you should obey it in its lusts."*
> *Romans 6:11-12*

John, the Apostle, knew this truth well because he wrote that the one who is truly born again does not sin (1John 3:6; 9)! The language here is very strong and confident and indeed it surprises many as on the other hand, in the same letter, he also states that if we say we do not sin we lie and the truth is not in us (1John 1:8). So, what did he really mean? He meant that the person that has come to the cross and has appropriated what happened there does not sin habitually. That is, sinful habits, actions and practices do not have a hold on us; we have been freed of their grip and power and can live in a way that pleases God. All of this is because "His seed", the very life of Christ, is in us (1 John 3:9). We must learn to trust the power of Jesus in us. I know that we have already examined this truth but some truths need constant repetition before we get them and this truth is vital to our daily walk with Jesus. Jesus saves to the uttermost (Hebrews 7:25)! This is why John also writes that the way we live as Christians is characterized by righteousness:

> "If you know that He is righteous, you know that everyone who practices righteousness is born of Him."
> 1 John 2:29

So, Paul had it right when he exhorted the readers of his Roman letter to count on the life of Jesus in them to fully transform them. He put it this way:

> "Therefore, brethren, we are debtors-not to the flesh, to live according to the flesh. For if you live according to the flesh you will die; but if by the Spirit you put to death the deeds of the body you will live."
> Romans 8:12-13

To Learn to Walk in Perfection

The cross, by virtue of reconciling us to God, has the power to fully transform our lives. In fact we are to see ourselves as already sinless and seated with Christ in heaven (Ephesians 2:4-6). The Spirit of God within us helps us to walk this position out in time and this is a process called sanctification. Our calling is to make our heavenly position of perfection an earthly reality. Or, to put it another way, we are to close the gap between what God says we are and what we actually are on earth. Paul acknowledged this when he stated that he presses forward toward "the upward call of God in Christ Jesus" (Philippians 3:12-14). That is, he is ever moving forward to have Christ's perfection of character established in his life. This was Paul's daily pursuit and, as he embraced it, he recognized that he had not yet fully attained his goal but he was getting close to it.

> "Not that I have already attained, or am already perfected; but I press on, that I may lay hold of that for which Christ Jesus has also laid hold of me."
> Philippians 3:12

Having said this, it is also true that we can be perfect! Paul clearly taught this but it has to be explained in that he did not mean that in this life we can attain to sinless perfection. The perfection Paul had in mind can be defined as, staying at the place of Christ-like transformation to which the Holy Spirit has brought us. It does not mean that one is a perfect reflection of Christ's character. No, it means that to the degree to which one has positively responded to the transforming light and power of Christ and is living in it; to that degree one is perfect! Paul put it this way:

"Therefore let us, as many as are perfect, have this mind; and if in anything you think otherwise, God will reveal even this to you. Nevertheless, to the degree that we have already attained, let us walk by the same rule, let us be of the same mind."
Philippians 3:15-16

When we walk in the power of God's transforming light and stay in God's transforming light, never going back, it is then that we are perfect. God holds us accountable only for the light that we have received. Paul acknowledges that not all Christians understand this and that in time God will make it clear to them but the bottom line is, "to the degree that we have already attained, let us walk by the same rule". We should never slide back into old habits and practices that God in Christ has delivered us from. Rather, like Paul, we forget those things which were behind and we press forward to those things which are ahead. The cross bought us a full deliverance and we should always move forward to appropriate it. The writer of the book of Hebrews understood this and wrote of it in these terms:

"Therefore, leaving the discussion of the elementary principles of Christ, let us go on to perfection, not laying again the foundation of repentance from dead works and of faith toward God...."
Hebrews 6:1

It's time for Christians to grow up, and indeed to wise up, and go forward to perfection!

To Learn the Ways of the Cross in Tribulation

"If anyone desires to come after Me, let him deny himself, and take up his cross and follow Me."
Matthew 16:24

The cross we shoulder every day is the one that applies the purchased blessings of Jesus' cross to our lives. Our cross challenges the "I principle" or "sin principle" in our lives every day. Paul refers to this as the "law of sin" (Romans 7:23). We do this by trusting the power of God in Christ to invade and transform our lives. We therefore, with God's help, put to death our old way of living and embrace the new ways of God. Because Jesus lives in us by the power of the Holy Spirit Paul commands us to change; this is not a suggestion.

> *"...if indeed you have heard Him and have been taught by Him, as the truth is in Jesus: that you put off, concerning your former conduct, the old man which grows corrupt according to deceitful lusts, and be renewed in the spirit of your mind, and that you put on the new man which was created according to God, in true righteousness and holiness."*
> *Ephesians 4:21-24*

Sometimes sin is so deeply rooted in our lives that we cannot change by simply being obedient to the word of God. It is for this reason that God allows us to walk through trials and tribulations. These have a habit of driving us to Christ as never before and so, through the ordeal of trials and tribulations, He is able to change us. This is not a blessed process but it is a necessary one and every true follower of Christ will be subjected to and trained by it and indeed, if we are not, we are not saved and are illegitimate! (Hebrews 12:8) In the end the power of Christ will have uprooted our stubborn evil ways and replaced them with that of Christ's. Peter encouraged the Christians of his day to submit to this process with patience:

> *"In this you greatly rejoice, though now for a little while, if need be, you have been grieved by various trials, that the genuineness of your faith, being more precious that gold that perishes, though it be tested by fire, may be found to praise, honor, and glory at the revelation of Jesus Christ."*
> *1 Peter 1:6-7*

> *"Therefore, since Christ suffered for us in the flesh, arm yourselves also with the same mind, for he who has suffered in the flesh has ceased from sin."*
> *1 Peter 4:1*

James, in his epistle, begins by encouraging the believers to hold steady in trials and not to get discouraged as in due time God will deliver them but not before He has effectively applied the cross to their lives. He puts it this way:

'My brethren, count it all joy when you fall into various trials knowing that the testing of your faith produces patience. But let patience have its perfect work, that you may be perfect and complete lacking nothing."
    James 1:2-4

Paul also appreciated the fact that trials and tribulations are the tools that God uses to apply Jesus' cross to our lives. That is, to not only impute righteousness to us but to impart righteousness to us. So he writes of this reality in these terms:

"And not only that, but we also glory in tribulations, knowing that tribulation produces perseverance; and perseverance, character; and character, hope. Now hope does not disappointment, because the love of God has been poured out in our hearts by the Holy Spirit who was give to us."
    Romans 5:3-5

Peter is a little more blunt because he writes:

"Therefore, since Christ has suffered for us in the flesh, arm yourselves also with the same mind, for he who has suffered in the flesh has ceased from sin."
    1 Peter 4:1

It is therefore clear that the way of the cross is a challenging way but we are all to submit to it, or as the writer of the book of Hebrews put it, be trained by it (Hebrews 12:7-11). In the end, by virtue of the power of God in us, we will be changed and people around us will take note that we have been with Jesus. (Acts 4:13)

To Learn to Walk in the Spirit
In the book of Romans Paul sets forth, in chapters seven and eight, the struggle that believers have in "finding their footing" in Christ. The cross has fully cancelled the power of sin in our lives but we struggle to appropriate it and so Paul gives personal testimony to his journey in this regard. He therefore cries out:

"For the good that I will to do, I do not do; but the evil I will not to do, that I practice. Now if I do what I will not to do, it is no longer I who do it, but

sin that dwells in me." "O wretched man that I am! Who will deliver me
from this body of death? I thank God-through Jesus Christ our Lord!..."
    Romans 7:19-20; 24-25

Paul then goes on to tell us that Jesus delivers us from in-dwelling sin by
our relationship with the Holy Spirit; that is, we are to walk in the Spirit
and consequently we will not give into sin or, as he puts it, to the flesh.

"There is therefore now no condemnation to those who are in Christ
Jesus, who do not walk according to the flesh but according to the Spirit."
    Romans 8:1

The question then is, how do we walk in the Holy Spirit? The answer,
according to Paul, is applying your mind in such a way that it agrees with
the truth of God's word. It is God's truth that sets you free and enables the
Spirit of God to work powerfully in your life. Our minds need to be made
subject to the word of God. So, Paul states, in confirmation of this:

"For those who live according to the flesh set their minds on the things
of the flesh, but those who live according to the Spirit, the things of the
Spirit. For to be carnally minded is death, but to be spiritually minded
is life and peace."
    Romans 8:6-7

It is then clear that, to walk in the Spirit, and thus apply to our lives all that
Jesus did for us on the cross, begins with our minds. We have to "want to"
change and then God changes us. When our minds stand on truth, that truth
explodes in our lives and transforms us. This is why Peter wrote that we
are to gird up the loins of our minds and follow Christ (1 Peter 1:13) and
Paul, writing to the Philippian Church, said that we are to train our minds
to dwell on good and godly things (Philippians 4:8-9). Christians today
need a radical commitment to the word of God and they need to support
this with lots of prayer and attendance at a good fellowship of God's people.
There is just no other way to walk in the Spirit and live out all the blessings
unleashed for us on the cross. In fact God only gives His Holy Spirit to those
who obey Him (Acts 5:32). This is precisely why it is so important to make
Jesus Lord of our lives.

Moreover, it is important to remember that on the cross Jesus reconciled us to God His Father and so by this redeeming work He brought us into real and vital union with the Father by the outpouring of His Spirit upon us (Acts 2:33). This Jesus called, "The "Promise of the Father" (Luke 24:49) and it constitutes our reception of the very powerful presence of God poured out upon our lives by the Holy Spirit. We call this the Baptism of the Holy Spirit and those who receive it are literally given a foretaste of heaven; a type of down-payment or deposit of heaven's reality. Paul wrote of this in these terms:

> *"In Him you also trusted, after you heard the word of truth, the gospel of your salvation; in whom also, having believed, you were sealed with the Holy Spirit of promise, who is the down payment of our inheritance until the redemption of the purchased possession, to the praise of His glory."*
> *Ephesians 1:13-14*

This baptism or infilling of the Spirit is promised to every blood washed believer and it constitutes the impartation of power enabling the Christ follower to walk more powerfully in God's truth (John 16:13) and to effectively be a witness for Jesus in the world (Acts 1:8). In short we cannot be all that God wants us to be without the life giving power of the Holy Spirit. Jesus well knew this and said as much on the great day of the Feast of Tabernacles when He cried out:

> *"...If anyone thirsts, let him come to Me and drink."..."But this He spoke concerning the Spirit, whom those believing in Him would receive; for the Holy Spirit was not yet given, because Jesus was not yet glorified."*
> *John 7:37; 39*

So, to sum it all up; when we trust in the finished work of Jesus on the cross, there is an impartation of God's life to us by the Holy Spirit whereby we are saved, become His children and can walk in the confidence of His transforming power (1 John 5:12), but; when we are baptized in the Spirit of God we enjoy an impartation of power whereby we effectively live for Him and serve Him in the world. We all need this and it is promised to all those who have embraced Christ as Savior.

> *"Then Peter said to them, "Repent, and let every one of you be baptized in the name of Jesus Christ for the remission of sins; and you shall receive*

the gift of the Holy Spirit. For the promise is to you and to your children,
and to all who are afar off, as many as the Lord our God will call."
    Acts 2:38-39

It is then most helpful to remember that when Paul commands us to be filled
with the Spirit he means it and in fact what he means is that we are to be
influenced by the Holy Spirit in the same way that the leaves and branches
of a tree bend to the direction of the wind when it blows upon them. The
Christian life is one of surrender and obedience and without our willingness
to give God both we shall remain carnal and immature and, sadly, there are
many Christians like this in our churches today. The Church at Corinth was
full of them prompting Paul to write:

"And I brethren, could not speak to you as spiritual people but as to carnal,
as to babes in Christ. I fed you with milk and not with solid food; for
until now you were not able to receive it, and even now you are still not
able; for you are still carnal."
    1 Corinthians 3:1-3

One Last Thing
The Bible clearly teaches that good works are not the grounds of our salvation
(Ephesians 2:8-9). These can never reach the perfection that God requires
and thus they are just "dead works" and have to be repented of (Hebrews
6:1). However, it is true that good works are indeed the evidence of a saved
life and of a life that is filled with the Spirit. Paul made this clear time and
time again and we should as well. Our faith is not entirely a professing faith
but rather one that is living and demonstrated. We must live differently to
the world and because of the power of the cross of Jesus unleashed in us
we must "turn the world upside down" (Acts 17:6). It is our good works of
service, kindness, caring and sharing that demonstrate the reality of Christ
in us. Paul, in writing to Titus put it this way:

"...looking for the blessed hope and glorious appearing of our great God and
Savior Jesus Christ, who gave Himself for us, that He might redeem us
from every lawless deed and purify for Himself His own people, zealous
for good works."
    Titus 2:13-14

In fact, according to Paul, once saved by the grace of God alone we are
to live a life of good works that indeed God has called us to before time

began:

> *"For we are His workmanship, created in Christ Jesus for good works,*
> *which God prepared beforehand that we should walk in them."*
>   *Ephesians 2:10*

The true Christ follower should demonstrate His relationship with God by living a life of good works. Indeed, as we read in Paul's exhortation to Titus, we are to be "zealous for good works." This is not possible unless we have Jesus living in us and demonstrating His life and power through us. We need Christians like this and truly God is looking for them. We must change our world by great acts of kindness and love. Again Paul writes:

> *"And let our people also learn to maintain good works, to meet*
> *urgent needs, that they may not be unfruitful."*
>   *Titus 3:14*

So here Paul brings us back to the idea of "fruitfulness." Jesus said that true Christians would be known by their fruit bearing and that this in effect means that a Christian tree will bring forth Christian fruit (Matthew 7:15-20). This fruit is the fruit of the Spirit and it is the abiding evidence that the cross of Jesus has impacted a life and changed it. The verse below gives us an understanding of what this fruit looks like.

> *"But the fruit of the Spirit is love, joy, peace, longsuffering, kindness, good-*
> *ness, faithfulness, gentleness, self control. Against such there is no law."*
>   *Galatians 5:22*

CHAPTER 4

According to the Pattern

"But Christ came as High Priest of the good things to come, with the greater and more perfect tabernacle not made with hands, that is, not of this creation. Not with the blood of goats and calves, but with His own blood He entered the Most Holy Place once for all, having obtained eternal redemption."
Hebrews 9:11-12

When Moses went up Mt Sinai, to receive the Law of God, he was also given a blueprint of exactly how to build the wilderness Tabernacle of meeting (Exodus 25:9). This blueprint was in fact a plan that would result in a structure being built on earth that would be a scaled replica, copy or model, if you wish, of a Tabernacle that, too this very day, exists in heaven. According to scripture the heavenly Tabernacle has an altar from which a burning coal was applied to Isaiah's life in order to cleanse him from sin; it has a holy place and a Holy of Holies, wherein dwells an Ark and Angels proceed from it as they go out into the world at the bidding of the God of Israel. Most important of all, it is the dwelling place of God.

"Then one of the Seraphim flew to me, having in his hand a live coal which he had taken with the tongs from the altar. And he touched my

mouth with it and said: "Behold, this has touched your lips; your iniquity is take away, and your sin purged."
Isaiah 6:6-7

"After these things I looked, and behold, the temple of the tabernacle of the testimony in heaven was opened. And out of the temple came the seven angels having the seven plagues, clothed in pure bright linen, and having their chests girded with golden bands."
Revelation 15:5-6

So then, this heavenly Tabernacle is real and it is herein that God dwells in light unapproachable and full of glory (1 Timothy 6:13-16). This is no replica or model; it is indeed the holy House of God's real presence; the very nerve center of the universe. Thus God told Moses that he was to reflect heaven on earth by building a Tabernacle into which, once built and consecrated by blood sacrifice, would be placed the glory of God's presence.

"And you shall raise up the tabernacle according to its pattern which you were shown on the mountain."
Exodus 26:30

"Therefore it was necessary that the copies of the things in the heavens should be purified with these, but the heavenly things themselves with better sacrifices than these"
Hebrews 9:23

Of note then is the fact that the very events described by the book of Revelation are orchestrated from this glorious heavenly Tabernacle. This, the book of Revelation emphasizes time and time again. This custodian of God's eternal presence and power cannot be fully comprehended because the glimpses we have of it in scripture are just too amazing but limited. It is a "greater" Tabernacle that rests upon what appears to be a sea of sparkling glass and in the Holy of Holies, upon this sea, is the Ark and a throne of such splendor that no human mind can fully grasp or appreciate it (Revelation 4:1-6). Above all, it is a place of indescribable perfection, beauty and holiness. The latter is measured by the character of God which is His glory and Angels constantly refer to this glory by crying out, "Holy, Holy, Holy is the Lord God Almighty (Isaiah 6:1-3)." There is no unrighteousness in this glorious Tabernacle, not even a smidgen of it and nothing unrighteous can dwell or enter there. Only those who are inherently like God can appear in this holy court! Sadly then for thousands and thousands of years no man ever entered this glorious chamber because all had sinned and had fallen short of the glory of God (Romans 3:23). But all of this changed in 33 AD when a perfect man once again entered the Tabernacle of Heaven and stood before the throne of God and this, all because of His death on the cross! To understand this we must consider the following:

A Perfect Sacrifice
Immediately after His resurrection Jesus entered the perfect heavenly Tabernacle and there, before God His Father, He placed His blood on the Mercy Seat of the Ark.

> *"But Christ came as High Priest of the good things to come, with the greater and more perfect tabernacle not made with hands, that is, not of this creation. Not with the blood of goats and calves, but with His own blood He entered the Most Holy Place once for all, having obtained eternal redemption."*
> *Hebrews 9:11-12*

This sacrifice became perfect and once for all because it was made by One who Himself was perfect and sinless and who died and rose again and entered the heavenly Tabernacle for us and as us. He thus, by His blood poured out on the cross, the very symbol of His perfect life, paid the price for our past, present and future sins. This He did for every person on earth (Hebrews 2:9; 2 Corinthians 5:14-15) and if accepted, by real repentance and faith in Him, we too are declared righteous as He is righteous and so, covered by His perfection, we too can enter the very throne room of the heavenly Tabernacle. Indeed we are encouraged to do this boldly!

> *"Let us therefore come boldly to the throne of grace, that we may obtain mercy and find grace to help in time of need."*
> *Hebrews 4:16*

Actually, the picture here presented to us by the book of Hebrews is dramatic to say the least because a perfect Man, clothed in blood, stood before the veiled Holy of Holies of the heavenly Tabernacle and then, just as the veil on earth in the "Copy Tabernacle" was split from the top to the bottom, so the eternal heavenly veil was split, in the same way from the top to the bottom, allowing the Son of Man to enter the very chamber of God's holy presence as us! Scripture captures this scene when it states:

> *"Then the temple of God was opened in heaven and the ark of His covenant was seen in His temple."*
> *Revelation 11:19*

A Perfect Intercessor

Christ's heavenly and priestly intercession has chiefly to do with pleading before His Father, for and on behalf of God's children on earth, the merits of His once for all blood sacrifice for them on the cross. This first of all means imputing His righteousness to them and also imparting His transforming power to their lives. However, secondly, it also means that He brings His Father's aid and care to their lives because He is acquainted with their weakness, troubles and grief. Jesus is a faithful High Priest in terms of intercession and not in terms of a perpetual sacrifice because this He accomplished once for all on the cross two thousand years ago. We may say then that Christ's heavenly ministry of intercession consists of mediating between God and men, securing for sinful men access to God and fellowship with Him. (1 Timothy 2:5) Christ exercises His High Priestly function in heaven, but it rests wholly upon the death, which He died once for all on earth.

When we boldly approach this glorious throne room, covered by the blood of Christ, to find mercy and grace in our time of need, we really do not know how to pray because of the crippling effect that sin has had upon our minds. We tend then to ask amiss (James 4:3) but Jesus, by His intercession in that Holy Place, "straightens out" our sincere but misguided prayers by entreating the Father to act on our behalf in the best way possible because His blood makes us perfect and fully accepted before Him. God our Father knows nothing of our weakness but His Son does, as He was as a man tempted in all points as we are, yet without sin. He is then a faithful High Priest on our behalf! The writer of the book of Hebrews declares:

> *"For Christ has not entered the holy places made with hands, which are copies of the true, but into heaven itself, now to appear in the presence of God for us."*
> *Hebrews 9:24*

And,

> "Therefore He is also able to save to the uttermost those who come to
> God through Him, since He always lives to make intercession for them."
> *Hebrews 7:25*

And,

> Seeing then that we have a great High Priest who has passed through the
> heavens, Jesus the Son of God, let us hold fast our confession. For we do
> not have a High Priest who cannot sympathize with our weaknesses, but
> was in all points tempted as we are, yet without sin."
> *Hebrews 4:14-15*

Yes, Jesus intercedes before His Father for each one of us every day by making sense of our weak prayers and circumstances and appealing to God to answer and address them in the best way possible. The answer may not be what we expected but it will be for our good. We have to trust in God's sovereignty in this because we know that He is holy and good and only has our best interests in mind. Paul knew this truth and so penned these words in his letter to the Church at Rome:

> "Who is he who condemns? It is Christ who died, and furthermore
> is also risen, who is even at the right hand of God, who also makes
> Intercession for us."
> *Romans 8:34*

These prayers of ours are brought to Jesus at the right hand of God by the Holy Spirit who lives in us and Who has been poured out upon us. He takes our weak and ignorant prayers and brings them to Jesus who, by His blood and intercession, turns them into what they should be. How blessed we are and what a marvelous encouragement to keep on praying. Again Paul writes:

> "Likewise the Spirit also helps in our weaknesses. For we do not know
> what we should pray for as we ought, but the Spirit Himself makes
> intercession for us with groanings that cannot be uttered. Now He
> (Jesus) who searches the hearts knows what the mind of the Spirit is,
> because He makes intercession for the saints according to the will of God"
> *Romans 8:26-27*

We have here a beautiful picture of the Holy Spirit searching our hearts with Christ and not only understanding our sincere prayerful cry but also correcting our misguided perception of what God our Father should do for us. He brings our prayers to Christ, who acquainted with our pain and weakness, presents them to His Father in the way that they would best serve our interests and become thereby an expression of the perfect will of God for our lives! We truly have a wonderful High Priest in heaven. To put it bluntly, we may not like the way our prayers are answered but we must remember that we do not know how to pray and the answer we get will be God's perfect will for us. Paul again reinforces this truth when he writes:

> *"And we know that all things work together for good to those who love*
> *God, to those who are the called according to His purpose."*
> *Romans 8:28*

These my friends are marvelous truths surrounding the blessings unleashed upon us by Jesus' death on the cross. The writer of the book Hebrews speaks at length about these and in response to them, in order to help us appropriate them, calls upon us to:
Draw near to God all the time with hearts that are full of faith and lives that are clean; having been washed with the word of God. We must live devotional lives that are rich in prayer and in the reading of God's word.

Hold fast the confession of our glorious hope. We must not let life's troubles discourage us and thereby tempt us to withdraw from Christ's love for us.

Be mindful of our fellow believers by encouraging them also as they journey with us upon this narrow way and by urging them to attend the regular meetings of the faithful...and,

Be expectant about Christ's soon return. The "Day" of His coming is indeed approaching and this blessed hope keeps our hearts right before God and our gaze upon heaven.

> *"Therefore, brethren, having boldness to enter the Holiest by the*
> *blood of Jesus, by a new and living way which He consecrated for*
> *us, through veil, that is, His flesh, and having a High Priest over the*
> *house of God, let us draw near with a true heart in full assurance*
> *of faith, having our hearts sprinkled from an evil conscience and*

*our bodies washed with pure water. Let us hold fast the confession of our
hope without wavering, for He who promised is faithful. And let us consider
one another in order to stir up love and good works, not forsaking the
assembling of ourselves together, as is the manner of some, but exhorting
one another, and so much the more as you see the Day approaching."*
    Hebrews 10:19-25

A Perfect Judge

*"For we must all appear before the judgment seat of Christ, that each
may receive the things done in the body According to what he has done,
whether good or bad."*
    2 Corinthians 5:10

Given the great and marvelous grace of God flowing toward us Jesus will bring us all into judgment. For the believer this will not be
about his entrance into heaven but rather an assessment of his life on
earth that, once concluded, will determine the place of privilege and
function that he will enjoy and occupy in the eternal kingdom of God.

*"According to the grace of God which was given to me I have laid the
foundation and another builds on it. But let each one take heed how he
builds on it. For no other foundation can anyone lay than that which
is laid, which is Jesus Christ. Now if anyone builds on this foundation
with gold, silver, precious stones, wood, hay, straw, each one's work will
become clear; for the Day will declare it, because it will be revealed by
fire; and the fire will test each one's work, of what sort it is. If anyone's work which he has built on it endures, he will receive a reward. If
anyone's work is burned, he will suffer loss; but he himself will be saved,
yet so as through fire."*
    1 Corinthians 3:10-15

However, for the Christ rejecting unbeliever there will be a terrifying judgment to come since it will unleash upon him the vengeance of God (Hebrews
10:26-31). They have twice rebelled against God; once in Adam and secondly
by rejecting Christ's finished work on the cross for them. Now God has no
alternative other than to cast them into hell! So, again the writer of the book
of Hebrews states:

"And it is appointed for men to die once, but after this the judgment..." Hebrews 9:27

And in the book of Revelation we read:

"Then I saw a great white throne and Him who sat on it, from whose face the earth and the heaven fled away. And there was found no place for them. And I saw the dead, small and great, standing before God, and the books were opened. And another book was opened, which is the book of Life. And the dead were judged according to their works, by the things which were written in the books. The sea gave up the dead who were in it, and Death and Hades delivered up the dead who were in them. And they were judged, each one according to their works. Then Death and Hades were cast into the lake of fire. This is the second death. And anyone not found written in the Book of Life was cast into the lake of fire."
    Revelation 20:11-15

However, there is also a present judgment flowing over the nations of the world. This judgment has repentance in mind and the intended purpose of bringing the nations to Christ, in order to save them from the great and final judgment that will send Christ rejecters to hell (Revelation 20:11-15). God is not willing that any should perish (2 Peter 3:9), and so this "present judgment" is dispensed by Angels who proceed to this holy work from the perfect and glorious Tabernacle in heaven. Christ's work on the cross demands that God employ all means possible to retard wickedness in the world and give the people of this world an opportunity to repent and be saved.

"After these things I looked, and behold the temple of the tabernacle of the testimony in heaven was opened. And out of the temple came the seven angels having the seven plagues, clothed in pure bright linen, and having their chests girded with golden bands."
    Revelation 15:5-7

Sadly, even as "present judgment" flows over this world humanity continues to love darkness more than it does light and will therefore not repent. They twice reject God and thereby spurn His love for them; a love that is so great that it sent His very unique and only Son to the cross for them. So scripture testifies to this by stating:

"And men were scorched with great heat, and they blasphemed
the name of God who has power over these plagues; and they did not
repent and give Him glory."
  Revelation 16:9

My friends, the cross towers over history and shines with the grace and love of God in Christ for a sinful world. We cannot escape it and it calls upon us all to embrace it and live out in our lives all that it imparts to us. If we do this we will one day enter a Tabernacle, not made with hands, where eternal life, made real by the very presence and fellowship of God, will be our inheritance. Be assured of this; very shortly Jesus will step out of the glorious Tabernacle of heaven and descend again to the earth to gather His eternal family to Himself. On that Day we will all marvel at His magnificence but His robe will still be dipped in blood!

"Now I saw heaven opened, and behold a white horse. And He who sat
on him was called Faithful and True, and in righteousness He judges
and makes war. His eyes were like a flame of fire, and on his head were
many crowns. He had a name written that no one knew except Himself.
He was clothed with a robe dipped in blood, and his name is called The
Word of God."
  Revelation 19:11-13

CHAPTER 5

The Gnostic Cross

"Now the Spirit expressly says that in latter times some
will depart from the faith, giving heed to deceiving spir-
its and doctrines of demons, speaking lies in hypocrisy, hav-
ing their own conscience seared with a hot iron..."
1 Timothy 4:1-2

"Beware lest anyone cheat you through philosophy and empty
deceit, according to the tradition of men, according to the ba-
sic principles of the world, and not according to Christ."
Colossians 2:8

"For many walk, of whom I have told you often, and now tell
you even weeping, that they are enemies of the cross of Christ:
whose end is destruction, whose god is their belly, and whose
glory is in their shame-who set their mind on earthly things."
Philippians 3:18-19

This, for me, is one of the most important and significant chapters that I have
written in years. A corrupt Gospel is infiltrating the mainstream evangelical church and its appeal lies in the fact that it is promising believers a new
power and authority that the church has never seen or experienced before.
All of this is based on special revelation knowledge that the preachers of this
message claim to have received. This is a form Gnosticism and it effectively
robs the believer of the blessings and power of the cross. It is in fact not
new but it is very dangerous and it is being promoted by leaders from the

so called, "Emerging Church" and the neo-Pentecostal movement. It is also becoming so "regular" now that if you challenge it you are considered out of step with God. I therefore submit this teaching to you as a warning lest you be carried away with a doctrine that will "tickle your ears" and deceive you (2 Timothy 4:3).

Definition

The Gnostic Gospel is that idea that a preacher, at a given point in time, has special revelation knowledge that when shared with God's people has to be immediately accepted in order for the blessings promised by it to be received. This means that the spiritual gifts, blessings and authority that flow from Jesus' finished work on the cross are made inaccessible to the believer until a preacher releases them. Failure to act in the moment designated by the preacher will disinvest the hearer of the blessings promised by him. The buzz word used by these false teachers is, **"Impartation."**

A more general definition is that Gnosticism is, a religious orientation advocating revelation knowledge as the way to release a person's spiritual element. Jesus, in his message to the Seven Churches of Asia expressed His hatred for this practice:

> *"But this you have, that you hate the deeds of the Nicolatians, which I also hate."*
> *Revelation 2:6*

The Nicolatians were a group of leaders in the early Church who were exercising spiritual power over the laity (congregational members). They were abusive, controlling and manipulative.

True Preaching

True preaching will always have the cross central to its proclamation and it will serve the truths surrounding the cross by calling upon its hearers to repent and make Jesus Lord of their lives. Paul emphasized this time and time again:

> *"For I determined not to know anything among you except Jesus Christ and Him crucified."*
> *1 Corinthians 2:2*

"But God forbid that I should boast except in the cross of our Lord Jesus Christ, by whom the world has been crucified to me, and I to the world."
   Galatians 6:14

"For Christ did not send me to baptize, but to preach the gospel, not with wisdom of words, lest the cross of Christ should be made of no effect."
   1 Corinthians 1:17

True preaching will also remind the believers in Jesus that God in Christ gave them everything they need "for life and godliness" 2000 years ago when Jesus died and rose again from the dead (2 Peter 1:3). God can give us nothing more because, as Paul affirms in his letter to the Ephesian Church, He has "blessed us with every spiritual blessing in the heavenly places in Christ" (Ephesians 1:3). Paul's statement is in the past tense and this means that God can give you nothing more as He has given you everything He has in Christ. In short, God's "more box "is empty and Christians who are called out in meetings to get more of God are just deceived. The fact is, God wants more of you! Jesus died to get God out of Heaven into man and this is why the veil in the temple was split from the top to the bottom when Jesus' redemptive sufferings ended. (Matthew 27:51) Paul knew that Christians would not easily understand this truth and thus, once again, in his Ephesian letter he writes:

"Therefore I also, after I heard of your faith in the Lord Jesus and your love for all the saints, do not cease to give thanks for you, making mention of you in my prayers: That the God of our Lord Jesus Christ, the Father of glory, may give to you the spirit of wisdom and revelation in the knowledge of Him, the eyes of your understanding being enlightened; that you may know what is the hope of His calling, what are the riches of the glory of His inheritance in the saints...,"
   Ephesians 1:15-18

It will be noted that Paul's prayer is that we should understand, not what we can get from God, but rather what He can get from us! God, by Christ, wants His inheritance in us. God wants more of us and this means that we walk with Him in surrender, obedience, patience, prayer, service and fellowship. In short we embrace those godly pursuits that give God access to our lives. The Bible calls this picking up your cross daily and following Christ (Luke 9:23). This is a daily joy, privilege and discipline. The seeking of instant encounters with God in a meeting driven by a Gnostic preacher will not give God His inheritance in us. It is the daily pressing in to all that Jesus purchased for us on the cross that brings us into the riches released to us by the cross 2000 years ago. True preaching declares the truths of God's word and allows the Holy Spirit to bring these to the hearts of the hearers. After Peter preached on the day of Pentecost we read that, "Now when they heard this they were cut to the heart, and said to Peter and the rest of the apostles, "Men and brethren, what shall we do?" (Acts 2:37) True preaching does not drive the sheep, it leads them!

This in turn means that all the blessings God has for us in Christ can be appropriated at anytime; even when shopping in a super-market! True preaching will serve Christ by telling the truth and it will not suggest that God's blessings are dependent upon responding to a preacher and his special revelation knowledge at a moment in time. True preaching will also recognize and declare that, after repentance and faith in Christ's finished work on the cross, the believer has to be baptized in water, filled with the Spirit, placed in a local church and conformed to the image of Christ. This is our holy calling and nothing more.

> "And He Himself gave some to be apostles, some prophets, and some pastors
> and teachers, for the equipping of the saints for the work of the ministry.
> Till we all come to the unity of the faith and of the knowledge of the Son of
> God, to a perfect man, to the measure of the stature of the fullness of Christ."
> Ephesians 4:11-12

It will be noted that gift ministries are given to the people of God in order to bring them to Christ's image or fullness. Their "equipping of the saints" is with this end in mind only (See also Romans 8:29-30). This is very important because the Gnostic preachers are now telling us that by revelation and apostolic gifting our calling is to take over the cities and nations of the world and rule them but, by contrast, Jesus said, "My kingdom is not of this world" (John 18:36). To support their error they routinely twist scripture, violate its context and thereby deceive the people of God. This is a very serious matter; for instance they will have you believe, by their special revelation, that the Church in the end time will be infused with a power that the Church of all ages did not have. A "Super Christian" is going to emerge who will be anointed to govern cities and nations and they falsely reference Ephesians

5:27 as proof of this. In their scheme of things, Jesus will not return until the Church, led by its apostolic leadership takes this place of authority. This is a lie, it deflects people from picking up their cross and Paul rebuked this lie in his first letter to the Corinthians:

> *"For who makes you differ from another? And what do you have that you did not receive? Now if you did indeed receive it, why do you boast as if you had not received it? You are already full! You are already rich! You have reigned as kings without us-and indeed I could wish you did reign, that we also might reign with you!"*
> *1 Corinthians 4:7-8*

Here Paul rebukes them for claiming a position and place of authority that God in fact has never given them. In the church or present age the people of God walk in humility and weakness recognizing that our weakness and imperfection precludes us from taking the position of dominion that God once gave to perfect Adam! However, we do see Jesus at the right hand of God, who by His incarnation and death on the cross, has begun a work of redemption in our lives. This work will only find its completion when Jesus comes again and then, and only then, will we reign with Him over the cities and nations of the world (Revelation 2:26-27). Now at this time, like Paul, we are "as men condemned to death; for we have been made a spectacle to the world, both to angels and to men". We are fools for Christ's sake because we are weak and dishonored! (Hebrews 2:8-9; 1 Corinthians 4:9-10). No, there will be no super empowered Christian at the end of the age and preachers who claim this nonsense must be and should be ignored. They are enemies of the cross.

False Preachers
These strut around the platform "dispensing the holy water" of their Gnostic gospel by claiming special revelation that has to be embraced at the moment they designate. If refused the people of God are told that they will forfeit this time of God's opportunity and blessing. This results in an altar call frenzy that is stirred up by the preacher that sees God's people desperate to grab the blessings promised in the moment. All of this is a gross distortion of the Christian faith and yet it is becoming so main stream that the people of God cannot recognize this. I recently attended a conference where the preacher promised, by revelation given only to him, that if the congregation did as he

told them at that moment they would receive new authority in their nations and within twelve months untold financial riches. Those who would not respond, as he desired, would be left spiritually destitute. This is nonsense and no one should be exploited like this in the house of God. Jesus weeps! It's time for the new money changers to be cleansed from the Temple of the Holy Spirit, the house of the living God. Here below is another example of this false Gnostic gospel; it will be noted that the preacher, who happens to be a prominent so called apostolic leader, gives a revelation based word in 2015 that denies everything that Jesus accomplished on the cross:

"I went into my little hidden office and the Lord began impressing me with the significance of the month of November. This is a month of unprecedented access to the Throne of God to erase the trace of the accuser in your life. This is the month the enemy loses hold of you and relinquishes his power to hinder. Why? Because this is when the ladder of heaven, like Jacob's ladder, is let down out of heaven and grace lifts you, even by the activity of angels, empowering you to see and to ascend into the very presence of God. The Lord would have you do this-even in your weakness-so that your weakness can be exchanged with new indomitable strength.

Access is granted to you. You are called to come into this place before His face, to stand in grace and occupy the space assigned to you before His throne. Your voice is needed at the throne of grace. It may be that your voice in this place is the key to many others running their race. Their success impacts your success. Be open to the prayers God gives you for others this month.

You will be given very accurate premonitions of people and things which you can pull and put to use like the smooth stone David used from the brook before slaying Goliath. This means God is giving you specific words of knowledge and insight into the future so you can pray your way into the places God has ordained for your feet to walk and pray into your possession the things that God has put within the metro of your authority.

You are going to cross over into your inheritance and the cycles of the past will break. This is the in and out lifestyle-the call to "go out and come in" to God's presence..."

It will be noted from this so called revelation that:

1. November 2015 is the month in which believers can get special access to God's throne. Actually believers gained access to God's throne the very day they surrendered their lives to Christ. They have no need for a so-called "Jacob's ladder" to give them standing before God. Jesus' blood spilt 2000 years ago on the cross did this once and for all (Romans 5:1-2).

2. November 2015 is the month in which the Devil's influence over believer's lives will be broken. This too is nonsense as the Devil was defeated 2000 years ago on the cross (Colossians 2:13-15). Believers who walk with Jesus have been freed from the Devil's influence from the day that they first believed.

3. November 2015 is the month a "new ladder" to heaven will be given to the believer. By the blood of Christ we come boldly into the presence of God all the time (Hebrews 10:19-20).

4. November 2015 is the month when the gifts of the Holy Spirit will be available to the people of God in a new way. This too is nonsense as when Jesus rose from the dead He gave gifts to men by the presence and power of the Holy Spirit who He poured out upon them (Ephesians 4:7-8).

Actually let me say it again, all of this is just nonsense because it was in April AD 33, 2000 years ago, that Jesus died on the cross of Calvary and once for all purchased all these things for us! God is in no way withholding them from us. Actually, to the contrary, He is waiting for us to fully appropriate them.

Scripture everywhere warns that the end time church will be infiltrated by these spiritual imposters:

> *"But there were also false prophets among the people, even as there will be false teachers among you, who will secretly bring in destructive heresies, even denying the Lord who bought them, and bring on themselves swift destruction. And many will follow their destructive ways, because of whom the way of truth will be blasphemed. By covetousness they will exploit you with deceptive words..."*
> *2 Peter 2:1-3*

The "Altar Call" is a mechanism that these new Gnostic cross preachers are exploiting. Actually, the altar call phenomenon is a relative new comer to the church's order of service. In its modern form it was popularized by the great evangelist of the nineteenth century, Charles Finney. Billy Graham also made good use of it and both of these evangelists, with Peter the Apostle, employed it as a way in which people could respond to the proclamation of the Gospel. This is good; but the modern day habit of using it to dispense spiritual blessings to the people of God has exalted the preacher, impoverished the people of God by denying their personal priesthood and taught them to expect "instant things" from God. By contrast the people of God are blessed and built up in their faith only as they learn to walk with Christ daily and follow Him (Acts 2:42). Christians need to learn how to "walk in Christ" (Ephesians 4:1). If they need prayer for anything they should call for the elders/leaders of the Church to pray for them. (James 5:13-15) Take note, the preacher doesn't call them out, they call the preacher out! They should be dealt with lovingly and in a probing manner since unconfessed wickedness and sin could be at the root of their problem. These things cannot be sorted out at an altar call but sadly the altar call has morphed into a tool by which Gnostic Preachers routinely abuse the people of God by playing on their emotions. Oral Roberts, the famous Pentecostal evangelist realized, to his credit, that a lot of what was happening at the altar call in his great tent meetings was psychosomatic, or a change of state only induced for a short time by intense emotional responses to the preaching. He thus withdrew from the practice except where it was used to call people to repent and make Christ their Lord.

Paul recognized that the message of false preachers had an appeal in that it promised the people of God all sorts of blessings and who doesn't want these? The Corinthian Church was being infused with these preachers and why would it not be true today? He therefore wrote:

> "But I fear, lest somehow, as the serpent deceived Eve by his craftiness, so your minds may be corrupted from the simplicity that is in Christ. For if he who comes preaches another Jesus whom we have not preached, or if you receive a different spirit which you have not received, or a different gospel which you have not accepted-you may well put up with it."
>   2 Corinthians 11:3-4

Conclusion

A true preacher is an Under Shepherd of Jesus, the Great Shepherd, and so he will rest Jesus' flock and never drive them. He will love them, care for them and defend them from wolves (Acts 20:17-31) and he will proclaim the truth of the cross in the power of the Holy Spirit all the while trusting Jesus to effectively apply it to people's lives. Today the wolves of the Gnostic Gospel are everywhere and we need to be aware of it and forearmed to avoid them. We should take seriously Paul's admonition to the Elders of Ephesus when he said:

> *"For I know this, that after my departure savage wolves will come in among you, not sparing the flock. Also from among yourselves men will rise up, speaking perverse things, to draw away the disciples after themselves."*
> *Acts 20:29-30*

Paul's antidote for this attack against the flock is to exhort the people to continuously live in the word of God and thereby to have their lives changed, built up and blessed.

> *"So now, brethren, I commend you to God and to the word of His grace, which is able to build you up and give you an inheritance among all those who are sanctified."*
> *Acts 20:32*

James gives the same advice:

> *"Therefore lay aside all filthiness and overflow of wickedness, and receive with meekness the implanted word, which is able to save your souls."*
> *James 1:21*

Preaching is always good and required but at the end of the day we are all believer priests and we have to individually appropriate all that Christ Jesus has done for us on the cross. It is he that endures to the end who will be saved; whether that "end" is by death or by the second coming of our Lord.

CHAPTER 6

Preachers of the Cross

"For I determined not to know anything among
you except Jesus Christ and Him crucified"
1 Corinthians 2: 2

"And He said to them, "Go into all the world and preach the gospel
to every creature."
Mark 16:15

The Call to Preach the Gospel

The word gospel means good news in that it brings the message of what Jesus did on the cross for the world to the world. He having died on the cross for our sins, as our representative and substitute means, as we have pointed out time and again in this book, that we are freed from the consequences of our sins, from the very curse of God and from the dominion of the Devil. This is very good news as those saved or delivered in this way are reconciled to God and enter into eternal life with Him. Only God by Jesus Christ could do this for us and so we are the recipients of God's unmerited grace, love and mercy. This is the message that we are to take to the world. Paul knew this and in fact, because he had experienced the saving power of Jesus' name, considered himself a debtor to the world. He owed them the message of the cross and would feel guilty before God if he kept it to himself.

"I am a debtor both to Greeks and to barbarians, both to the wise and to
the unwise. So, as much as is in me, I am ready to preach the gospel to
you who are in Rome also."
Romans 1:15- 15

It goes then without saying that every Christian should shoulder this responsibility to preach the gospel to their friends, family and community. This is not the sole responsibility of the so-called professional clergy.

The Servant of the Gospel
The servant of the gospel is the law. By the law we mean the moral or majestic law otherwise known as the Ten Commandments. This law constitutes a written description of the character of God. To break it then, as we all have, is to offend the very character of God or glory of God and subsequently to bring ourselves under the curse of the law or wrath of God. The unrepentant sinner has this curse hanging over his life every day and if he refuses to turn to Christ by repentance and faith in what He did for him on the cross, he will be forever cursed in hell! John the apostle picked up on this when he wrote:

> *"He who believes in the Son has everlasting life; and he who does not believe the Son shall not see life, but the wrath of God abides on him."*
> *John 3:36*

This is an awful state to live in and therefore we must urgently preach the gospel to everyone and to do this effectively we must begin by preaching the law because this is the means by which the Holy Spirit will convict the ungodly of their sins and of the curse that hangs over their lives. Jesus said that when the Holy Spirit comes into the world, "He will convict the world of sin, and of righteousness, and of judgment" (John 16:8). No one comes to Christ because they are lonely, have financial problems or have broken relationships. No, we come to Christ because we have offended the character of God and have thus become blasphemers, liars, cheats, thieves, adulterers, murderers, fornicators, idolaters and God haters (1 Corinthians 6:9-10) It is only when we preach the law of God that sinners, by the Holy Spirit, will come under conviction of these things and move toward Christ for deliverance from the curse of the law. This is precisely why Paul said:

> *"Therefore the law was our tutor to bring us to Christ, that we might be justified by faith."*
> *Galatians 3:24*

And again;

"Now we know that whatever the law says, it says to those who are under the law, that every mouth may be stopped, and all the world may become guilty before God. Therefore by the deeds of the law no flesh will be justified in His sight, for by the law comes the knowledge of sin."
    Romans 3:19-20

Today preachers preach anything but the law as they consider the message of the law to be too harsh and negative. The result is sinners are not getting saved and the true message of the cross is being hidden from them. The true preacher of the cross must not be afraid to wound and offend the ungodly because his trust is not in the approval of men but in the power of the Holy Spirit to convict the sinner of his sinful ways, to break his hard heart and bring him to repentance. Some will reject the message and even resist the message but the message of the cross must be preached to every creature. Paul wrote that on the cross Jesus became a curse for us and thereby delivered us from the curse of the law. How then shall the unsaved be delivered from the curse of the law if they know nothing about the law?

"Christ has redeemed us from the curse of the law having become a curse for us (for it is written, "Cursed is everyone who hangs on a tree"), that the blessing of Abraham might come upon the Gentiles in Christ Jesus, that we might receive the promise of Spirit through faith."
    Galatians 3:13-14

Yes truly, the law is the "servant of the gospel" and until we pick it up and rightly use it, as Paul and John and Charles Wesley did, we shall not attract the convicting power of the Holy Spirit to our meetings and our preaching will be powerless and weak.

The Messenger of the Gospel

The messenger of the cross is Himself a recipient of the marvelous grace and mercy of God and therefore with compassion and love he must:

- Hold the sinner accountable for his sinful actions. Once again we must note that God does not love the sinner and hate his sins. No, God hates the sinner and holds him fully accountable for what he has done. The unrepentant sinner will learn this lesson well at the end of time when God casts him into hell (Revelation 20:15). The truth is, God hates the sinner and loves him at the same time and we have to understand this not in human terms but in the knowledge that God is "holy love" and therefore must be just and the justifier of the ungodly (Romans 3:26).

- Hold the law of God over sinners' lives because this alone will convict them of their sins and of the wrath of God to follow. Jesus alone by His cross delivers us "from the wrath to come"(1 Thessalonians 1:10).

- Hold up the cross of Jesus before sinners as the only answer to their sinful dilemma. In Christ's awful sufferings the sinner must see what he rightfully deserves and will receive if he doesn't repent and put his trust in Jesus. Jesus gave His dear sinless life as "ransom for sinners" (Mark 10:45). To pay a ransom for someone means to buy his or her freedom. The question then is; to whom did Christ pay the price to free us from our sins? The answer is, to His Father in heaven! Jesus' death was a propitiation, meaning that first and foremost He satisfied God's holy demands against us on the cross. John put it this way:

"In this is love, not that we loved God, but that He loved us and sent His Son to be the propitiation for our sins."
  1 John 4:10
The messenger of the cross must be well acquainted with these things and preach them powerfully.

- Hold before the sinner the awful reality of spending eternity in hell should he die without Christ. Today preachers give all sorts of reasons why they should not preach on hell. The truth is, they do not want to offend people and so the consequences of an eternity without Christ are routinely watered down and very often Hell is only referred to in passing or as "that other place." In fact hell is a place of outer darkness, of unrelenting fire, torment, pain and of eternal separation from God. The messenger of the cross must stand at the crossroads of life as it were holding back sinners from going to hell. (Proverbs 24:11-12)

- Hold before the sinner God's command to repent and make Jesus Lord of his life (Acts 17:30-31). After Jesus' obedience, by going to the cross for each and every one of us, God exalted Him to His right-hand as Lord (Philippians 2:5-11). Jesus must become Lord of our lives because it is only by complete submission to His authority over our lives that we can be transformed, by his saving power, into His image. We do not grow into accepting His Lordship over our lives as this notion leaves "wiggle room" to persist in our ungodly ways. No we repent and by faith in what Jesus did for us on the cross we receive Him as Lord. This was the message of the apostolic preachers as reflected in the book of Acts. (Acts 2:36) Jesus, Himself, challenged His hearers about this very matter when He said;

"But why do you call Me 'Lord, Lord' and not do the things which I say?"
John 6:46

• Hold before the world a clean heart and life. The messenger of the gospel must be authentic and must himself live out and thus demonstrate what he is preaching. This gives his message credibility and power. Paul knew this well and constantly called upon his hearers to follow him as he followed Christ (1 Corinthians 11:1). We would do well to note his words in 1 Thessalonians 3:12

"For our exhortation did not come from error or uncleanness, nor was it in deceit. But as we have been approved by God to be entrusted with the gospel, even so we speak, not as pleasing men, but God who tests our hearts. For neither at any time did we use flattering words, as you know, nor a cloak of covetousness-God is witness. Nor did we seek glory from men, either from you or from others, when we might have made demands as apostles of Christ. But we were gentle among you, just as a nursing mother cherishes her own children affectionately longing for you, we were well pleased to impart to you not only the gospel of God, but also our own lives, because you had become dear to us. For you remember, brethren, our labor and toil; for laboring night and day, that we might not be a burden to any of you, we preached to you the gospel of God. You are witnesses, and God also, how devoutly and justly and blamelessly we behaved ourselves among you who believe; as you know how we exhorted, and comforted, and charged every one of you, as a father does his own children, that you should walk worthy of the God who calls you into His own kingdom and glory."

We would do well to carefully examine this passage because it gives us good insight into what it means to be a true messenger of the cross. Today we constantly witness the spectacle of false preachers whose only real interest it appears is to exploit the people of God financially. Their gospel does not "attack" sin, call for repentance and warn of the very real fires of hell. Neither does it hold up before the world the glories of the cross. Paul also encountered these preachers and wrote of them in these words:

> *"For many walk, of whom I have told you often, and now tell you even weeping, that they are enemies of the cross of Christ: whose end is destruction, whose god is their belly, and whose glory is in their shame- who set their mind on earthly things."*
> *Philippians 3:17-18*

Let us humbly strive to be the true messengers of the cross.

CHAPTER 7

Some Final Thoughts

As I bring this book to an end I want to turn our thoughts to the tragic and yet glorious events that surrounded the crucifixion of Jesus as the writer of the book of Hebrews saw them. Understanding these events transforms the cross from an instrument of execution to one of a glorious and only pathway to heaven. Paul saw the implications of what Jesus did on the cross as something amazing, deeply humbling and worth telling to the whole world. The message of the cross here presented by the writer of the book of Hebrews is equally good news indeed and no passage underlines this more than the first two chapters of the book.

Jesus, through whom God made the worlds

"God, who at various times and in various ways spoke in time past to the fathers by the prophets, has in these last days spoken to us by His Son, whom He has appointed heir of all things, through whom also He made the worlds; who being in the brightness of His glory and the express image of His person, and upholding all things by the word of His power, when He had by Himself purged our sins, sat down at the right hand of the Majesty on high..."
Hebrews 1:1-3

The writer's focus here is upon the glorious credentials of Jesus that give great importance to His speaking. In short Jesus' message must be heard because of Who He is and what He did for all of us on the cross. He is perfect God and perfect man; a Godman who was not born into the world but begotten (John 1:14). Jesus pre-existed with God from all eternity, is His express image and was the instrument by which His Father created the worlds. He not only created the worlds but also upholds them by the "word of His power!" (Colossians 1:15-17) It is this One that purged or wiped away all our sins on the cross. That is, our past, present and future sins have been removed from our lives thus freeing us from their awful consequences and enabling God to see us as sinless and perfect in Christ. Our past sins were deliberate but, as Christians, our present and future sins are by default or unintentional. (Hebrews10:26-27) If we then confess them "He is faithful and just to cleanse us from all unrighteousness." (1John 1:9)

This passage is then like a new Genesis in that once again God is speaking through a "New Adam" Who, if listened to, will begin a new family on the earth. A family who will hear His voice, repent of their sins, walk in righteousness and ultimately eat from the "Tree of Life" (Revelation 2:7). By contrast the writer also warns that those who ignore "the speaking of God" in Christ will not escape the wrath of God!

> *"For if the word spoken through angels proved steadfast, and every transgression and disobedience received a just reward, how shall we escape if we neglect so great a salvation, which at the first began to be spoken by the Lord, and was confirmed to us by those who heard Him."*
> *Hebrews 2:2-3*

Jesus, crowned with glory and honor

> *"For in that He put all in subjection under him (mankind), He left nothing that is not put under him. But now we do not yet see all things put under him. But we see Jesus, who was made a little lower than the angels, for the suffering of death crowned with glory and honor, that He, by the grace of God, might taste death for everyone."*
> *Hebrews 2: 8-9*

The intention of God in creation was that humankind would rule over, or have dominion over, the earth. The original man, before the fall, was a superman! His calling was to tame the world, give it order and allow it to thrive and become even more beautiful. This was God's plan for men and women. We cannot even begin to imagine the capacity that we potentially have and that has been marred and lost by our rebellion against God in Adam. Quoting from Psalm eight the writer of the book of Hebrews laments the fact that humankind never fully entered into its destiny; "We do not yet see all things put under him (humankind)." However, we do see Jesus in this place of dominion and His death for every person on the earth guarantees a place of full restoration to all those who repent and accept Him as Lord. The writer exclaims, "He tasted death for everyone" meaning that, potentially, all of mankind has an opportunity to recover its place of dominion. Now, in this life, we are embracing the life of Christ in order to overcome the effects that sin has had upon our lives but one day, when Jesus comes, we will be like Him and with Him we will rule the worlds! (Revelation 2:26-28; 3:21) His death is the only pathway back to the place that God originally intended for us. It is with this hope in our hearts that we too pick up the cross daily and follow Him.

> *"Then He said to them all, 'If anyone desires to come after Me, let him deny Himself, and take up his cross daily, and follow Me."*
> *Luke 9:23*

Jesus, through death destroyed the Devil

> *"Inasmuch then as the children have partaken of flesh and blood He Himself likewise shared in the same, that through death He might destroy him who had the power of death, that is, the devil, and release those who through fear of death were all their lifetime subject to bondage...Therefore in all things He had to be made like His brethren, that He might be a merciful and faithful High Priest in things pertaining to God, to make propitiation for the sins of the people."*
> *Hebrews 2:14-17*

Strangely the power of the Devil over our lives was the character of God. God is just and holy and consequently sin, rebellion and wickedness separate us from His life, presence and protection. We were thus "cut loose" from God's care and left as prey to the Devil and his demons. (Ephesians 2:1-3) We could only return to God if these demands of His character could be met. This we could not do but Jesus, by virtue of His sinless life, satisfied the demands of God's character fully on our behalf when He died on the cross. This is what the word "propitiation" means. The way is now open for all peoples to return to God in Christ and to be forgiven of their sins and the Devil cannot stop this! The Devil's jail house has been plundered, the gates are unlocked since Jesus has the keys and we can all walk free! (Revelation 1:18) Our Father in heaven now invites us "home" and welcomes us just as the father welcomed his wayward son in the parable of the Prodigal Son (Luke 15:11-32). It is this message of the cross that we have to preach and which the Devil seeks to keep blinded from the world. (2 Corinthians 4:3-4) This is precisely why our understanding of the cross is so very important. Make no mistake, the Devil is constantly seeking to undermine, dilute and corrupt the message of the cross and sadly, in many respects, he has accomplished this.

This then, in a nutshell, is the story of Jesus' cross and the one that we should focus upon all the days of our lives. Meditate on these wonderful things and make them your own and then tell them to the world.

Concluding Remarks

> *"Now all things are of God, who has reconciled us to Himself through Jesus Christ, and has given us the ministry of reconciliation, that is, that God was in Christ reconciling the world to Himself, not imputing their trespasses to them, and has committed to us the word of reconciliation."*
> *2 Corinthians 5:18-19*

The death of Jesus is more than amazing as it not only validates the holy character of God and the great love that He has for His world but it also reminds us that God became flesh, dwelt among us as a perfect man and then laid down His life for each one of us as an atonement for our sins. In this sacrificial way God upheld the goodness of His character and extended love and mercy to us all. All of this is quite frankly mind blowing and the historical cross of Jesus is most definitely the greatest event in history. God the Creator was in Christ reconciling the world to Himself.

Jesus was eminently qualified to redeem us, as He had to be God and a perfect sinless man to achieve this. He was both and so becoming our substitute on the cross "He bore the sin of many" and then rose from the dead. Death could not hold him and in fact He willingly laid His life down for us and then took it up again from the dead. This was the power of His indestructible life and He Himself affirmed it:

> "Therefore My Father loves Me, because I lay down my life that I may take it again. No one takes it from Me, but I lay it down Myself. I have power to lay it down, and I have power to take it again. This command I have received from My Father."
> John 10:17-18

The resurrection is the final proof that all our sins have been atoned for on the cross and that we by repentance and faith in what Jesus did for us on the cross can enter into that eternal life that God planned for us before time began (2 Timothy 1:9). This is precisely why the apostolic preaching of the cross laid great emphasis upon the resurrection of Jesus. It was the resurrection that gave glorious meaning to Jesus' death and we are called to preach on the cross in the light of it. Peter declared it thus:

> "Him, being delivered by the determined purpose and fore knowledge of God, you have taken by lawless hands, have crucified, and put to death; whom God raised up, having loosed the pains of death, because it was not possible that He should be held by it."
> Acts 2:23-24

> "To you first, God, having raised up His Servant Jesus, sent Him to bless you, in turning away every one of you from your iniquities."
> Acts 3:26

And Paul said,

> "Truly, these times of ignorance God overlooked, but now commands all men everywhere to repent, because He has appointed a day on which He will judge the world in righteousness by the Man whom He has ordained. He has given assurance of this to all by raising Him from the dead."
> Acts 17:30-31

Yes truly God was in Christ reconciling the world to Himself and so when we accept Jesus as Lord into our lives we are accepting God Himself into our hearts (John 1:12). We are all made with a body, a soul and a spirit (1 Thessalonians 5:23) and it is in the spirit of man that God in Christ takes up residence by the Holy Spirit and so the great work of redemption, transformation and restoration begins. Scripture affirms that it is, "Christ in us the hope of glory" (Colossians 1:27), that we are temples of the Holy Spirit (1 Corinthians 6:19) and that our Father in heaven lives in us (John 14:23). This then is a remarkable testimony to the oneness of the Godhead and it is no wonder then that Paul once gave the following benediction:

> *"The grace of the Lord Jesus Christ, and the love of God, and the communion of the Holy Spirit be with you all. Amen."*
> *2 Corinthians 13:14*

Epilogue

We all know what John 3:16 states in that, "God so loved the world that He gave His only begotten Son, that whoever believes in Him should not perish but have everlasting life." This verse clearly designates Jesus' mission; He gave His perfect, sinless life on the cross so that we can be delivered from the consequences of our sins and covered with His righteousness. This is the very good news of the gospel.

However, how many of us know what 1 John 3:16 has to say? Let us read these words carefully:

"By this we know love, because He laid down His life for us. And we also ought to lay down our lives for the brethren."

So here John the Apostle somewhat reverses (not contradicts) the truth of John 3:16 in that that those who have come to Christ, by repentance and faith in His finished work on the cross, are called upon to be saviors too. That is, they must be prepared to lay down their lives for the community of faith. Not to save them from their sins but to save them from life's perils, trials and challenges!

This giving of our lives for one another definitely implies martyrdom but not exclusively in that we are in fact to lay down our best interests, resources, talents and energy for those in the Body of Christ. Only a life that under-stands the meaning of the cross can do this.

"Let nothing be done through selfish ambition or conceit, but in lowliness of mind let each esteem others better than himself. Let each of you look out not only for his won interests, but also for the interests of others. Let this mind be in you, which was also in Christ Jesus, who being in the form of God, did not consider it robbery to be equal with God, but made Himself of no reputation, taking the form of a bond-servant, and coming in the likeness of men. And being found in the appearance as a man, He humbled Himself and became obedient to the point of death, even death on a cross." Philippians 2:2-8

May it be so, Selah.